THE PURPLE BOOK

Answer Key

EDWIN R. RIDEOUT THD., MDIV.,MA.,B.TH

Contact author via email:

edwinrhoda@gmail.com

www.edwinrideout.com

Facebook: www.facebook.com/edwin.r.rideout/

Linkedin: www.linkedin.com/in/edwinrideout

X (Twitter): twitter.com/edwinrideout

Instagram: www.instagram.com/edwin.r.rideout/

Phone (780)742-3933

I was helped to publish my book by: Hemingway Publishers

About The Compiler

Rev. Dr. Edwin R. Rideout is the Author of *Generous Living: Mysterious Joy* and numerous articles. With over 30 years of full-time ministry experience, Dr. Rideout has dedicated his life to pastoral leadership, discipleship, and helping others encounter the transforming power of God's Word. He and his wife, Rhoda, serve together in ministry, mentoring leaders and guiding people toward spiritual maturity.

Connect with Edwin @

edwinrhoda@gmail.com www.edwinrideout.com

Facebook: www.facebook.com/edwin.r.rideout/

Linkedin: www.linkedin.com/in/edwinrideout

X (Twitter): twitter.com/edwinrideout

Instagram: www.instagram.com/edwin.r.rideout/ Phone (780)742-3933

This guide is not affiliated with or endorsed by the original authors or publisher of The Purple Book.

About This Companion Guide

This *Answer Key* was carefully compiled to accompany *The Purple Book: Biblical Foundations for Building Strong Disciples* by Rice Broocks and Steve Murrell. Designed for small groups, new believers, and spiritual mentors, it provides Scripture-based answers to reinforce biblical understanding and inspire faithful living.

The Purple Book is a foundational discipleship tool. The results of its use have been remarkable, producing genuine spiritual growth and a hunger for God's Word throughout the church community. This Answer Key is born out of that lived experience, with the prayer that it will be a valuable guide for churches and believers everywhere.

Acknowledgments

First, I give all glory and thanks to Jesus Christ, the central figure of the biblical story, the One who has called, saved, and continues to build His church. Without Him, none of this would be possible.

I am deeply grateful to the authors of *The Purple Book*, whose clear and faithful teaching of God's Word has impacted my life and the lives of many around the world. Their work has been a rich resource in helping believers lay strong foundations for their faith.

To my dear team at the Family Christian Centre—Rhoda, Alex, Andy, Beverly, Dawn, Grace, Holly, Melissa, Merissa, Natasha, Riza, Ryley, and Stephen—your support, encouragement, and partnership have been invaluable. Each of you has played a unique role in helping me bring this project to fruition. I thank God for your hearts, your wisdom, and your steady presence along this journey.

I would also like to thank Trevor Sacrey, my first disciple under this project. As a new believer, his hunger for truth and genuine desire to grow in Christ inspired me to begin and complete this Answer Key. His journey has been a beautiful reminder of why solid, biblical discipleship matters so deeply.

May God use this work to strengthen many in their walk with Him, for His glory and the advancement of His kingdom.

Table of Contents

Chapter 1
Sin and Salvation

Lesson One:
The Original Story

1. What was creation like in the beginning? Genesis 1 -

    - **vs. 10** - God made dry land and seas. He saw that it was good.

    - **vs. 12** - Plants and trees grew, each making seeds. God saw that it was good.

    - **vs. 18** -The sun ruled the day; the moon and stars ruled the night. God saw that it was good.

    - **vs. 21** - God made fish to fill the seas and birds to fill the skies. He saw that it was good.

    - **vs. 25** - Animals of all kinds lived on the land. God saw that it was good.

2. How many commands did God give Adam & Eve? Genesis 2:17 - One. Not to eat from the Tree of the Knowledge of Good and Evil.

3. What was God's command to the first human beings? Genesis 2:16-17 - "You may freely eat from every tree in the garden except the tree of the knowledge of good and evil."

4. How did Adam and Eve respond to God's command? Genesis 3:6-7 - Adam and Eve disobeyed God's command by eating the forbidden fruit from the tree of the knowledge of good and evil. The serpent tempted Eve. She saw the fruit as desirable and ate it. She also gave some to Adam, who ate it as well.

5. In light of this, do you think you would have responded differently?

____

____

____

____

6. Who tempted Eve? Genesis 3:1 - Satan, in the form of a serpent.

7. How did Adam and Eve react after their eyes were opened and they realized they were naked? Genesis 3

    - **vs. 7** - They made their clothes.

    - **vs. 8** - They hid from God.

    - **vs. 10** - They lied, and Adam said he was afraid because he was naked.

8. Why do you think they responded in this manner? - They knew they had disappointed God. They also experienced spiritual death.

9. How did God respond to Adam & Eve's sin? Genesis 3:8-9 - God sought them out. This shows God's initiative to engage with them despite their disobedience, reflecting His justice and desire for restoration.

APPLICATION & REFLECTION QUESTION

What did you learn from this section, and how will you apply it to your life?

____

____

____

____

Lesson Two:
The Results of Sin

1. What state does the Bible describe us as being in? Ephesians 2:1 - Spiritually dead.

2. Why, ultimately, is our sin so serious to God? Leviticus 11:44 - Our sin is ultimately so serious to God because it directly opposes His holy nature and purpose for humanity.

3. What does iniquity do to our relationship with God? Isaiah 59:1-2 - Sin (iniquity) causes a barrier between humanity and God. Though God remains all-powerful and able to save, our iniquity severs the relationship. This separation excludes us from His presence, guidance, and fellowship.

4. Describe sinful humanity's desperate condition. Romans 3:9-20, 23 - Sinful humanity's desperate condition is described as utterly pervasive, leaving all people guilty before a holy God and incapable of saving themselves.

5. Describe the impact sin has on our hearts. Jeremiah 17:9 - Sin makes the heart inherently deceitful. This means it is prone to self-deception, convincing us that our actions and desires are justified or reasonable when, in fact, they are not.

6. What are the wages of sin? Romans 6:23 - The wages of Sin are eternal death.

7. What does the Bible say happens after we die? Hebrews 9:27 - We appear before God to be judged for how we live our lives.

8. How does the Bible describe eternal judgment?

- Matt. 25:41- Eternal fire prepared for the devil and his angels.

- 2 Thess. 1:9-10 - Suffer eternal destruction, away from the presence of the Lord and His glory.

- Rev. 21:8 - Consigned to the fiery lake of burning sulphur - the second death.

9. What does Paul, the writer of Romans, call himself? Romans 7:24 - A wretched man.

APPLICATION & REFLECTION QUESTION:

What did you learn from this section, and how will you apply it to your life?

____

____

Lesson Three:
God's Solution for Sin- Jesus' Death and Resurrection

1. What is necessary for the forgiveness of sins? Hebrews 9:22 - The shedding of innocent blood.

2. How did God cover Adam & Eve's first sin? Genesis 3:21 - He clothed them with garments made of skins. This indicates that an innocent animal was slain.

3. How were unclean things made clean? Hebrews 9:22 - Almost everything was purified with blood under the Mosaic law.

4. Can the blood of animals ultimately take away our sins? Hebrews 10:4 - The blood of animals cannot remove sin.

5. Why would the promised Saviour be pierced? Isaiah 53:5 - He was pierced for our transgressions (sins).

6. How does the prophet Isaiah describe our healing? Isaiah 53:5 - His wounds heal us.

7. How did John the Baptist, the last great prophet before Jesus, introduce Jesus publicly? John 1:29 - "The Lamb of God," who takes away the sin of the world.

8. What did the prophet Isaiah predict God would do? Isaiah 53:6 - Place all our sins (iniquities) upon Jesus.

9. What does Jesus' blood- his sacrificial death- do for us?

   - Romans 5:9 - Justifies us [Declares us in good standing with God].

   - Ephesians 1:7 - Provides redemption [paid our debt].

   - Ephesians 2:13 - brought near to Him [our relationship restored].

   - 1 John 1:7 - Cleanses us from all sin.

   - Revelation 1:5 - Sets us free from the power of sin.

10. What did Jesus do for us on the cross?

    - 1 Corinthians 15:3-4 - He died for our sins

    - 2 Corinthians 5:21 - Took upon himself all our sins

    - Galatians 3:13-14 - He took the curse for our wrongdoing upon himself.

    - 1 Peter 2:24 - He carried the load of our sin

11. According to the Bible, what makes Jesus unique so that he can do this for us?

    - John 1:18 - He is God's Son.

    - Colossians 1:15-20 - He created everything that exists in the universe.

- Hebrews 4:15 - He is our Great High Priest. He fully understands our weaknesses.

12. What is the significance of Jesus' resurrection? What if there was no resurrection? 1 Corinthians 15:14-19

   - vs. 14 - Our preaching and our faith are useless.

   - vs. 15 - We are misrepresenting God [being untruthful].

   - vs. 16 -If dead people never rise to a new life, then Christ did not rise after his death.

   - vs. 17 - We are still in our sins.

   - vs. 18 - The dead have no hope of being resurrected; they have perished.

   - Vs. 19 - If we only trust Him to help us in this life, we should be deeply saddened.

APPLICATION & REFLECTION QUESTION:

What did you learn from this section, and how will you apply it to your life?

____

____

____

____

Lesson Four:
Receiving God's Heart - A New Heart

1. What did God promise he would give his people? Ezekiel 36:26 - God pledged to His people a new heart and spirit.

2. What does God do when He rescues us from our state of spiritual death? Ephesians 2:4-6 - God makes us alive with Christ, raises us up, and seats us with Him in heavenly places [a position of spiritual influence].

3. What happens when we receive Jesus as Lord and Saviour? John 1:12-13 - We become children of God.

4. What did Jesus say must happen before we can enter the kingdom of God? John 3:3-7 - Jesus said we must be born again, born of water and the Spirit, to enter the kingdom of God [That means experiencing spiritual rebirth through God's Spirit].

5. What do the following passages tell you about being born again or born of God?

   - John 1:12-13 - When we receive him, we are born of God [in other words, God does all the work].

   - 1 Peter 1:23- We are given a new life that will never spoil [it is eternal].

   - 1 John 3:9 - When we're born of God, our desires change; therefore, we stop sinning [this is made possible by the Holy Spirit's help over time].

   - 1 John 4:7 - We love everyone when we are born of God.

6. What does Paul say about those who are "In Christ"? 2 Corinthians 5:17 - Paul says those who are "in Christ" are new creations; the old way of living has gone, and a new way of living has come.

7. What is the destiny of those "born of God"? 1 John 5:4 - They overcome the temptations of the world.

APPLICATION & REFLECTION QUESTION:

What would you do if someone could offer you a brand new start in life? Have you received God's gift of new life?

____

____

____

____

Lesson Five:
- Grace Through Faith

1. Is it possible to be saved by the good things we do—our "works"? How are we saved? Ephesians 2:8-9 - No, our works cannot save us. We are saved by grace through faith, a gift from God, not a result of our efforts.

2. Does God save us because of the good things we do? If not, why does he save us? Titus 3:4-5 - God does not save us because of our good deeds. He saves us because of His mercy.

3. What does God's grace teach the believer? Titus 2:11-12 - God's grace teaches the believer to say no to ungodliness and worldly passions and to live a life that pleases God.

4. Shall we continue to sin because of God's forgiveness and grace? Romans 6:15 - No, we should not continue to sin because we are under grace. That would show disregard for all that Christ has provided for us.

5. What are we created for as new Christians? Ephesians 2:10 - We are designed to do good works, which God prepared in advance of us being born for us to do.

6. What did Jesus say to those who believed in Him? Matthew 16:24 - Jesus said, "If you want to follow me, you must give up your way, accept the challenges that come with it, and stay close to me."

APPLICATION & REFLECTION QUESTION:

What did you learn from this lesson? How will you apply it to your life?

____

____

____

____

Chapter 2
Lordship and Obedience

Lesson One:
Jesus is Lord.

1. What did Peter (one of Jesus' disciples) proclaim about Jesus? Acts 2:36 - Peter announced that God declared Jesus both Lord (ruler) and Messiah (Saviour).

2. What did Paul write about Jesus? Philippians 2:6-11

   - vs.6 - Jesus, though equal to God, didn't use His power to His

   - advantage.

   - vs.7 - Instead, He gave it up, became a servant, and lived as a human.

   - vs.8 - He humbled Himself completely and obeyed God by dying on the cross.

   - vs.9 - God lifted Him to the highest place and gave Him a name above every other.

   - vs.10 - At His name, everyone will kneel—in heaven, on earth, and below.

   - vs.11 - Everyone will declare that Jesus is Lord, bringing glory to God.

3. What does Paul say we should do after we receive Jesus? Colossians 2:6 - Paul says we should continue to follow Jesus, stay strong, and develop our faith in Him.

4. What did Jesus say was the result of not obeying him? Luke 6:46-49

5. - Jesus said that not obeying Him is like building a house without a foundation—it will collapse when trouble comes.

6. According to Jesus, who will enter the kingdom of heaven? Matthew 7:21-23 According to Jesus, only those who do God's will will enter the kingdom of heaven.

APPLICATION & REFLECTION QUESTION

What did you learn from this lesson? How will you apply it to your life?

____

____

____

____

Lesson Two:
The Narrow Door

1. What does Jesus say about entering the kingdom of God? Matthew 7:13-14 - Jesus says entering the kingdom of God is like taking a narrow road. It's hard, and only a few find it, but it leads to life. The wide road may seem easy, but it ultimately leads to destruction.

2. How can we distinguish between genuine followers of Jesus and those who are not? Matthew 7:16 - Jesus says you can tell genuine followers by their actions, like recognizing a tree by the fruit it produces.

3. According to Jesus, what is the destiny of those who bear bad fruit? Matthew 7:19 - Jesus says those who live in ways that don't please God will face His judgment.

4. Centuries before Jesus was born, God gave his people the Law, summed up in the Ten Commandments. What are God's Ten Commandments? Exodus 20:1-17.

    - vs. 3 - Worship only God; have no other gods.

    - vs. 4-6 - Don't make or worship idols; God is a jealous God

    - who shows love to those who love and obey Him.

    - vs. 7 - Don't misuse God's name.

    - vs. 8-10 - Keep a Sabbath day by resting and honouring God.

    - vs. 12 - Honour your father and mother.

    - vs. 13 - Don't murder.

    - vs. 14 - Don't commit adultery.

    - vs. 15 - Don't steal.

    - vs. 16 - Don't lie or give false testimony.

    - vs. 17 - Don't covet (desire) what belongs to others.

5. What did Jesus say about those who disregard these laws?

    Matthew 5:17-19 - Jesus said that anyone who disregards these laws and teaches others to do the same will be least in the kingdom of heaven. But those who follow them and teach others will be great in the kingdom of heaven.

6. How did Jesus say we could sum up all of God's laws? Matthew 7:12 - God's laws can be summed up by treating others as we would want to be treated.

7. What is the difference between those who love Jesus and those who do not? John 14:15,23-24 - Those who love Jesus obey His commands, while those who do not love Him ignore His teachings.

8. What does Paul say must not be in our lives as believers? Ephesians 5:3-5 - Paul says there must not be sexual immorality, impurity, greed, obscenity, foolish talk, or crude jokes in our lives as believers.

9. What did Paul warn would happen to those who practice such things? Galatians 5:19-21 - Paul warned that those who practice such things will not inherit the kingdom of God.

10. What is the reason people live in sin and still think that they are Christians? 1 Corinthians 6:9-10 - People live in sin and still think they are Christians because they are deceived, not realizing that wrongdoers will not enter God's Kingdom.

APPLICATION & REFLECTION QUESTION

What did you learn from this lesson? How will you apply it to your life?

____

____

Lesson Three:
Lordship and Relationships

1. According to the Bible, what kind of people should we avoid altogether? 1 Corinthians 5:11 - The Bible says we should avoid people who claim to be Christians but live in sin.

2. In one letter, Paul mentions an alarming case of immorality. What did Paul say the church should have done? I Corinthians 5:1-2 - Paul said the church should have been saddened by the sin and removed the person from their group to deal with the situation seriously.

3. What did Paul say about "fellowship" with unbelievers? 2 Corinthians 6:14-16 - Paul said we shouldn't team up with unbelievers in close partnerships because righteousness and sin, or light and darkness, don't mix.

4. What does God command? 2 Corinthians 6:17 - God says we should separate ourselves from sinful ways, avoid what is wrong, and stay close to Him. He will be like a loving Father to us.

5. What does he promise in return? 2 Corinthians 6:18 - God promises that He will be our Father, and we will be His sons and daughters

6. How does John say we know we "have passed from death to life'? 1 John 3:14 - John says we know we've passed from death to life because we love others.

7. How many times did Jesus say we should forgive our brothers and sisters? Matt.18:21-22 - Jesus said we should forgive our brothers and sisters seventy-seven times, meaning we should always forgive.

8. As we live in love and unity with one another, what did Jesus promise would be the world's response? John 17:23 - Jesus promised that when we live in love and unity, the world will know that God sent Him and loves us.

9. What is the key to having this kind of unity? Philippians 2:3-4 - The key to unity is humility. Putting the interests of others above our own interests.

APPLICATION & REFLECTION QUESTION

What do you think it means to be in the world but not of the world? John 17:15-18

____

____

____

____

Lesson Four:
Can You Pass the Test?

1. What is the message that John proclaimed? 1 John 1:5 - John's message is that God is pure and perfect, with no sin or wrongdoing in Him at all.

2. What does John say about those who claim to have fellowship with God and yet continue to walk in darkness? 1 John 1:6 - John says if we say we're close to God but keep living in sin, we're not being honest.

3. What does the Bible say about people who claim to be Christians but do not follow God's commands? 1 John 2:3-4 - The Bible says people who claim to be Christians but don't follow God's commands are not living the truth.

4. What does God command?

    - **John 3:11** - God commands us to love one another.

    - **Matthew 22:34-40** - God commands us to love Him with all our heart, soul, and mind, and to love our neighbour as ourselves.

5. What does John say about those who claim to love God but hate their fellow believers? 1 John 2:9-11 John says that if someone says they love God but hate other believers, they still live in darkness and don't know what's right.How can we know the difference between "children of God" and "children of the devil"? 1 John 3:7- 10 - The children of God do what is right and love others, while children of the devil keep sinning and don't show love.

6. If we say we love God yet hate a brother or sister, what does the Bible say we are? (1 John 4:20) - We are liars.

APPLICATION & REFLECTION QUESTION

What did you learn from this lesson? How will you apply it to your life?

____

____

____

Chapter 3
Repentance and Baptism

Lesson Three:
What Shall We Do?

1. What did the prodigal son say to his father? Luke 15:21 - Father, I have sinned against heaven and before you. I am no longer worthy to be called your son.

2. What was the response of the Father? Luke 15:22-24 - The Father's response was to celebrate with joy, dressing his son in the best robe, giving him a ring, new sandals, and throwing a feast because his lost son had returned home.

3. What did Jesus say causes heaven to celebrate? Luke 15:7 - Jesus said heaven celebrates when one sinner repents more than ninety- nine righteous people who don't need to repent.

4. Who did Peter declare Jesus Christ to be? Acts 2:36 -Peter declared Jesus Christ to be both Lord and Messiah.

5. What did the people say in response to Peter's preaching? Acts 2:37 - The people responded to Peter's preaching by saying, "What shall we do?" They were deeply moved and wanted to know how to respond.

6. What did Peter say they should do? Acts 2:38 - Peter said they should turn away from their sins and be baptized in Jesus' name. Then God would forgive their sins and give them the Holy Spirit.

7. What did Peter say they would receive if they repented and were baptized? Acts 2:38 - Peter said they would receive forgiveness for their sins and the gift of the Holy Spirit.

8. Who did this promise apply to? Acts 2:39 – This promise is for everyone—for you, your children, and anyone else God calls, wherever they may be.

9. What else did Peter say? Acts 2:40 - Peter told them to change their ways, leave behind the wrong actions of their sinful generation, and choose to follow God to be saved

10. What happened to those who accepted the message? Acts 2:41 - Those who accepted the message, were baptized, and about 3,000 people were added to the group that day

11. Once they were added to the local body of believers, what did they do? Acts 2:42-46 - Once they joined the group of believers, they devoted themselves to the apostles' teaching, fellowship, the sharing of meals (including the Lord's Supper), prayer, and helping one another. They met regularly, shared what they had, and praised God with joyful hearts.

APPLICATION & REFLECTION QUESTION

What did you learn from this lesson? How will you apply it to your life?

____

____

Lesson Two:
Repentance - Turning From Sin

1. What message did Jesus preach? Mark 1:15 - Jesus preached, "The time has come. The kingdom of God has come near. Repent and believe the good news!"

2. What message should be preached in all nations? Luke 24:47 - The message of repentance and forgiveness of sins should be preached in all nations.

3. What happens when we repent and turn to God? Acts 3:19 - When we turn away from our sins and come to God, He forgives us and gives us a fresh start with His peace and grace.

4. What promise do we have from God when we repent of our sins? (1 John 1:9) - He will forgive our sins and cleanse us from the effects of our sinful lives.

5. What did Jesus say would happen if we didn't repent? Luke 13:2-5 - Jesus said if we don't turn away from our sins, we will face judgment.

6. Who does God command to repent? Acts 17:30 - God commands everyone, everywhere, to repent.

7. What did the apostle Paul say he was sent to do? Acts 26:18 - Paul said he was sent to open people's eyes, turn them from darkness to light, and from the power of Satan to God, so they could receive forgiveness of sins and a place among God's people.

8. What message did Paul say he preached? Acts 26:19-20 - Paul said he preached that people should repent, turn to God, and demonstrate their repentance by their actions.

9. How did Paul instruct his listeners on how to demonstrate their repentance? Acts 26:20 - Paul told his listeners, they could demonstrate their repentance by turning to God and doing deeds that show they have changed.

10. What should we do about our sins? Proverbs 28:13 - We should confess and turn away from our sins to receive mercy.

11. True repentance involves confessing sin, turning away from sin, and turning to God. What else is involved? Exodus 22:3 - True repentance also involves restitution—repaying or making things right for our wrongdoings.

12. Zacchaeus was a corrupt tax collector. Yet the opportunity of a relationship with Jesus inspired him to repent and make restitution for his sins. How did he propose to make restitution? Luke 19:8 - Zacchaeus proposed to give half of his possessions to the poor and repay anyone he had cheated four times the amount.

13. How did Jesus respond to Zacchaeus? Luke 19:9 – Jesus responded by saying, "Today salvation has come to this house because this man has shown true faith and is now part of God's family."

14. What leads us towards repentance? Romans 2:4 - God's kindness, patience, and mercy lead us toward repentance.

15. Part of repentance is being sorry for our sins. What are the two types of sorrow, and what do they produce? 2 Corinthians 7:10 - First, godly sorrow. Feeling genuinely sorry for sin because it offends God. This leads to repentance, a changed life, and salvation. The other is worldly sorrow, which is regret or guilt without turning to God. It leads to hopelessness and spiritual death.

16. Besides repentance, what else does Godly sorrow produce? 2 Corinthians 7:11 - Godly sorrow produces eagerness to make things right, a desire to clear yourself, indignation about sin, reverence for God, longing to do better, and a readiness to correct wrongs and pursue righteousness.

APPLICATION & REFLECTION QUESTION

What did you learn from this lesson? How will you apply it to your life?

____

____

____

____

Lesson Three:
Repentance - Turning to God

1. What did Paul say we must turn to when we turn from darkness? Acts 26:18 - Paul said we must turn to God's truth and power when we leave behind sin and darkness.

2. What was the result of the miraculous healing of a paralyzed man? Acts 9:35 - Everyone in the towns of Lydda and Sharon saw it and turned to the Lord.

3. What was the evidence the "Lord's hand" was with those who proclaimed Christ? Acts 11:21 - Many people believed and turned to the Lord.

4. Is simply saying you believe in God enough? James 2:19 - No, merely saying you believe in God is not enough. Even demons believe in God, and they tremble in fear. True faith is shown through actions.

5. What does the Bible say about faith without any corresponding works? James 2:26 - The Bible says that faith without works is dead, just like a body Without a spirit, it is dead.

6. What is the promise for those who truly believe? John 6:47 - The promise for those who genuinely believe that they will have eternal life.

7. What does the Bible say overcomes the world? 1 John 5:4-5 - Those who believe that Jesus is the Son of God, achieve victory over the world.

APPLICATION & REFLECTION QUESTION

What did you learn from this lesson? How will you apply it to your life?

____

____

____

____

Lesson Four:
Water Baptism

1. What happened to those who accepted Peter's Message? Acts 2:41 - Those who accepted Peter's message were baptized, and about 3,000 people were added to the group of believers that day.

2. What did the men and women who believed Philip's message do? Acts 8:12 - The men and women who believed Philip's message were baptized.

3. After hearing the good news about Jesus, what did the Ethiopian eunuch want to do? Acts 8:35-36 - After hearing the good news about Jesus, the Ethiopian eunuch wanted to be baptized.

4. Jesus told his disciples to make disciples of all nations. What did he say to do with those disciples? Matthew 28:19-20

    - **vs. 19** - Jesus said to baptize them in the name of the Father, the Son, and the Holy Spirit.

    - **vs. 20** - He said to teach them to obey everything He commanded and promised to always be with them.

5. Paul compares Christian baptism to a burial. To be buried, a person must first die. What must we die to before we can be baptized? Romans 6:1-4 - Paul says we must die to sin before baptism. Baptism symbolizes being buried with Christ and raised to live a new life.

6. The Israelites' passing through the Red Sea is a picture of baptism for us. Why were the Israelites fleeing from the Egyptians? Exodus 2:23; 3:7,9 - The Israelites were fleeing from the Egyptians because they were enslaved and oppressed, crying out to God for deliverance. God heard their cries and rescued them from their suffering and hardship.

7. What happened to the Egyptians? Exodus 14:22-28 - God caused the waters to return, drowning Pharaoh's army, chariots, andhorsemen, while the Israelites safely crossed on dry ground.

8. Paul says baptism is like a circumcision not done by human hands, but a circumcision done by Christ. What is put off during this spiritual circumcision? Colossians 2:11-12 - Paul says that during this spiritual circumcision, the sinful nature (or the "flesh") is put off. This happens when we are buried with Christ in baptism and raised through faith in God's power.

9. What did Peter say the flood water symbolized? 1 Peter 3:21 - Peter said the flood water represents baptism, which saves us not by washing our bodies but by showing we turn to God with a clean heart through Jesus' resurrection.

10. What is baptism a pledge of? 1 Peter 3:21 - Baptism is a pledge of a clean heart and a good conscience toward God.

APPLICATION & REFLECTION QUESTION

What did you learn from this lesson? How will you apply it to your life?

____

____

____

____

Chapter 4
The Holy Spirit and Spiritual Gifts

Lesson One:
Who is the Holy Spirit?

1. Who Is the Holy Spirit?

- John 14:16 - The Holy Spirit is the Advocate (Helper) sent by the Father to be with us forever.

- John 14:17 - The Holy Spirit is the Spirit of truth, who lives with believers and will be in them.

2. What are some ways the Holy Spirit helps the believer?

- Matthew 10:19-20 - The Holy Spirit gives believers the right words to say in difficult situations.

- John 14:26 - The Holy Spirit teaches and reminds believers of

- Jesus' teachings.

- John 16:13-14 - The Holy Spirit guides believers into all truth and glorifies Jesus.

- Acts 1:8 - The Holy Spirit gives believers the power(ability) to be witnesses for Christ.

- Romans 8:14 - The Holy Spirit leads and guides believers.

- Romans 8:15 - The Holy Spirit frees believers from fear and

- confirms their adoption as God's children.

- Romans 8:16 - The Holy Spirit assures believers that they are

- God's children.

- Romans 8:26-27 - The Holy Spirit assists believers in prayer and

- intercedes on their behalf according to God's will.

- 2 Timothy 1:14: The Holy Spirit fills us with grace and power.

APPLICATION & REFLECTION QUESTION

What did you learn from this lesson? How will you apply it to your life?

____

____

____

____

Lesson Two:
The Fruit of the Holy Spirit

1. How can we bring glory to the Father? John 15:8: By bearing much fruit and showing we are Jesus' disciples.

2. What happens to the branches that do not bear fruit? John 15:2: They are cut off from the vine and taken away.

3. What happens to the branches that bear fruit? John 15:2: They are pruned so they can bear even more fruit.

4. Why does the Father prune fruitful branches? John 15:2: To help them grow and produce more fruit.

5. Can we bear fruit by ourselves? John 15:4: No, we can only bear fruit if we remain in Jesus.

6. What must we do to bear spiritual fruit? John 15:4-5: Remain in Jesus, because apart from Him, we can do nothing.

7. What does it mean to "remain in the vine"? John 15:4-7: It means staying connected to Jesus through faith, obedience, and His Word.

8. List the fruit of the Spirit. Galatians 5:22-23 - The fruit of the Spirit is love, joy, peace, patience, kindness, goodness, faithfulness, gentleness, and self-control.

9. Which is the greatest? 1 Corinthians 13:13 - Love is the greatest.

10. Where does the Holy Spirit dwell? 1 Corinthians 3:16 - The Holy Spirit dwells in believers. we are God's temple(s).

APPLICATION & REFLECTION QUESTION

Do you see evidence of the fruit of the Spirit in your life? Which ones do you have? Which ones do you still need to develop?

____

____

____

____

Lesson Three:
Spiritual Gifts

1. List the "spiritual gifts" Paul mentions in Romans. Romans 12:6-8 -

   - **Prophecy** – Speaking God's message in alignment with faith.

   - **Serving** – Helping and meeting the needs of others.

   - **Teaching** – Explaining and applying God's truth clearly.

- **Encouragement** – Inspiring others to grow in faith and remain faithful.

- **Giving** – Sharing resources generously and willingly.

- **Leading** – Guiding others with diligence and responsibility.

- **Showing Mercy** – Demonstrating kindness and compassion cheerfully.

2. List the Leadership gifts God has placed in the church. Ephesians 4:11-12 -

  - **Apostles** – Pioneers and foundation layers for the church.

  - **Prophets** – Those who proclaim God's Word and guidance.

  - **Evangelists** – Those who share the Gospel and bring others to Christ.

  - **Pastors** – Shepherds who care for and guide the church.

  - **Teachers** – Those who instruct and help others grow in God's

  - **truth.**

3. List the "manifestations of the Spirit" that are given for the common good. 1 Corinthians 12:4-11 -

  - **Word of Wisdom** – Insightful guidance and application of knowledge.

  - **Word of Knowledge** – Knowing facts revealed by the Spirit.

  - **Faith** – Extraordinary trust in God's power.

  - **Gifts of Healing** – Miraculous ability to heal physical, emotional, or spiritual ailments.

  - **Working of Miracles** – Performing supernatural acts by God's power.

- **Prophecy** – Declaring God's message for encouragement or

- instruction.

- **Distinguishing Between Spirits** – Recognizing the spiritual source behind actions or messages.

- **Speaking in Different Tongues** – Speaking in languages not learned, empowered by the Spirit.

- **Interpretation of Tongues** – Understanding and explaining the meaning of tongues.

4. What attitude should we have regarding Spiritual Gifts? 1 Corinthians 14:1 - We should eagerly desire spiritual gifts, especially the gift of prophecy, to build up and encourage others.

5. What should be our motivation for desiring and using our spiritual gifts? 1 Corinthians 13:1-2 - Our motivation for desiring and using spiritual gifts should be love. Without love, even the most extraordinary gifts or abilities are meaningless.

6. What does Paul say about the gift of prophecy? 1 Corinthians 14-

    - vs. 1 - We should eagerly desire spiritual gifts, especially prophecy.

    - vs. 3 - Prophecy strengthens, encourages, and comforts others.

    - vs. 4 - Those who prophesy build up the church.

    - vs. 31 - Everyone can prophesy in turn, so all may learn and be encouraged.

    - vs. 39-40 - We should be eager to prophesy, ensuring everything is orderly and respectful.

7. What does Paul say about the gift of tongues? 1 Corinthians 14 -

    - vs. 2 - Speaking in tongues is directed to God and involves mysteries spoken by the Spirit, not understood by others.

- vs. 4 - Speaking in tongues builds up the individual, but prophecy builds up the church.

- vs. 5 - Paul desires everyone to speak in tongues but values prophecy more because it benefits the church unless the tongues are interpreted.

- vs. 13 - Those who speak in tongues should pray for the ability to interpret them.

- vs. 14 - When praying in tongues, the spirit prays, but the mind does not understand.

- vs. 15 - The spirit and the mind should be engaged in prayer and worship, balancing tongues and understanding.

- vs. 39-40 - Do not forbid speaking in tongues, but ensure everything is done in a fitting and orderly way.

8. What are we warned against doing?

    - **1 Thessalonians 5:19-20:** Don't hold back the work of the Holy Spirit or ignore prophecies.

    - **Ephesians 4:30:** Don't make the Holy Spirit sad by how you live, since He marks you as God's own for salvation.

9. What did Jesus promise would happen to the disciples when the Holy Spirit came on them? Acts 1:8 - Jesus promised that when the Holy Spirit came upon the disciples, they would receive power and become His witnesses to the ends of the earth.

APPLICATION & REFLECTION

Have you experienced the Spirit's power in your life? How? What did you learn from this lesson? How will you apply it to your life?

Lesson Four:
The Baptism in the Holy Spirit

1. What did John the Baptist promise Jesus would do? Matthew 3:11 - John the Baptist said Jesus would give people God's Spirit and power to change their lives.

2. How did Peter describe the Gentiles' encounter with the Holy Spirit? Acts 11:15-17 - Peter described the Gentiles' encounter with the Holy Spirit as being the same as what the apostles experienced at the beginning, saying the Holy Spirit came upon them just as He had at Pentecost.

3. What did Jesus tell his disciples they were to do after he ascended to heaven?

    Luke 24:49 - Jesus instructed them to stay in Jerusalem until God gave them the power of the Holy Spirit.

    Acts 1:4-5 - Jesus told them to wait for the Holy Spirit to fill them.

4. Read the following five accounts of people who received the Holy Spirit in the book of Acts. How did they receive the Spirit? Describe what happened when people in these accounts received God's Spirit.

    *   **Acts 2:1-6:** The Holy Spirit came with wind and fire, and people began speaking different languages.

    *   **Acts 8:14-19:** Peter and John laid hands on believers, and they visibly received the Holy Spirit.

- **Acts 9:17-19:** Ananias laid hands on Saul; he was filled with the Spirit, healed, baptized, and regained strength.

- **Acts 10:44-48:** While Peter preached, the Holy Spirit came on Gentiles, and they spoke in tongues and praised God.

- **Acts 19:1-6:** Paul laid hands on believers, and they received the Holy Spirit, spoke in tongues, and prophesied.

5. Who does the Father give the Holy Spirit to? Luke 11:13 - The Father gives the Holy Spirit to those who ask Him.

APPLICATION & REFLECTION QUESTION

Have you asked to receive God's Holy Spirit? What did you learn from this lesson? How will you apply it to your life?

____

____

____

____

Chapter 5
Spiritual Hunger and God's Word

Lesson One:
The Authority and Power of the Word

1. How does the Bible say the world was created? 2 Peter 3:5 - God created the Heavens and the earth by His word, and the earth was formed out of water and through water. It reminds us that God's power brought everything into existence.

2. What were the first followers of Jesus - his disciples - devoted to? Acts 2:42 - The first followers of Jesus were devoted to learning from the apostles, spending time together, sharing meals, and praying.

3. What were the top two priorities for the early church leaders? Acts 6:4 - The top two priorities for early church leaders were praying and teaching God's word.

4. What happened as "the Word of God" spread? Acts 6:7 - As the Word of God spread, the number of believers grew quickly, and even many religious leaders became followers.

5. What was "the word of the Lord" doing in Ephesus while Paul was there? Acts 19:20 - The word of the Lord was spreading widely and growing in influence.

6. How were the Scriptures initially given to us?

    - 1 Corinthians 2:13 - Taught by the Holy Spirit.

    - 2 Timothy 3:16 - Scripture was breathed out by God.

7. What does John say about "the Word"? John 1:1 - John says the Word was with God, the Word was God, and He created everything. Then the Word became human and lived among us— this is Jesus.

8. Who is "the Word"? John 1:14 - The Word is Jesus. He became human and lived among us.

9. What do the following passages teach us about God's word?

   - **Psalm 119:89** – God's Word stands firm forever.

   - **Psalm 119:160** – God's Word is entirely accurate and will neverchange.

   - **Isaiah 40:8** – People and things fade, but God's Word lasts forever.

   - **Isaiah 55:11** – God's Word always accomplishes His purpose.

   - **Matthew 24:35** – Heaven and earth will pass away, but God's Word will never disappear.

   - **John 17:17** – God's Word is truth and makes us holy.

10. What does the writer of Hebrews say about God's word? Hebrews 4:12 -God's Word is alive and powerful. It cuts deep into our hearts, revealing our thoughts and intentions.

11. What does Jesus say we will be judged according to on the last day? John 12:48 - Jesus says His words will judge us on the last day.

APPLICATION & REFLECTION QUESTION

What does God's Word mean to you? Spend time reflecting on this.

____

____

____

____

Lesson Two:
The Benefits of the Word

1. What was God's command to Joshua, and what was his promise if Joshua obeyed? Joshua 1:8 - God commanded Joshua to be strong and courageous, obey His law, and not turn from it. He promised that if Joshua obeyed, he would be successful, and God would be with him wherever he went.

2. Describe the person who meditates on God's word. Psalm 1:1-3 – A person who meditates on God's Word is blessed, strong, and fruitful—like a tree planted bywater, thriving in every season.

3. What are the Scriptures helpful for? 2 Timothy 3:16-17 - The Scriptures teach us what is true, correct us when we're wrong, guide us to do what is right, and prepare us to serve God.

4. How did Jesus overcome temptation and defeat the devil? Matthew 4:1-11 - Jesus overcame temptation by quoting Scripture and standing firm in God's truth.

5. How can God's people experience victory over sin?

- Psalm 119:9 - We can overcome sin by living by God's Word.

- Psalm 119:11 - remembering it and living according to its principles.

- List some of the ways God's word benefits the believer.

- Giving wisdom and understanding (Psalm 119:98-100).

- Guiding them like a light in the dark (Psalm 119:105).

- Bringing peace and keeping them from stumbling (Psalm 119:165).

- Bringing life and healing (Proverbs 4:20-22).

APPLICATION & REFLECTION QUESTION

What did you learn from this lesson? How will you apply it to your life?

____

____

____

____

Lesson Three:
Spiritual Hunger

1. What was David's greatest desire? Psalm 119:81 - David's greatest desire was to trust in God's word and find hope in Him.

2. How did the sons of Korah describe the condition of their souls? Psalm 42:1- The sons of Korah described their souls as thirsty for God, desiring Him like a deer longs for water.

3. What was the psalmist's attitude toward God's presence? Psalm 84:1-2,10 -The psalmist loved and longed for God's presence, saying that spending one day with God was better than a thousand elsewhere.

4. Who did Jesus say would be filled? Matthew 5:6 - Jesus said those who hunger and thirst for righteousness will be filled.

5. What do you think it means to "hunger and thirst for righteousness"? - It means intensely wanting to live God's way and do what is right.

6. What did David say about God's word and its importance?

    - Psalm 119:72 – God's Word is more valuable than riches.

    - Psalm 119:103 – God's Word is sweeter than honey.

    - Psalm 119:127 – God's Word is more precious than gold.

    - Describe Job's hunger for God's word? Job 23:12 - Job valued God's Word

    - more than his daily food. He depended on it entirely.

    - What did Jeremiah say about God's word? Jeremiah 15:16 - Jeremiah said he

    - took in God's Word, and it brought him joy and delight.

APPLICATION & REFLECTION QUESTION

What did you learn from this lesson? How will you apply it to your life?

____

____

____

____

Lesson Four:
Obedience

1. What happens if we only listen to the word? James 1:22 - If we only listen to the word but don't act on it, we deceive ourselves.

2. How does James describe those who only listen to the word without putting it into practice? James 1:23-24 - James describes them as people who look in a mirror, see themselves, but forget what they look like as soon as they walk away.

3. What happens to those who hear and act on the word? James 1:25

   - Those who hear and act on the word will be blessed in what they do.

4. How did the Bereans respond to the preaching of Paul and Silas? How often did they read and study the scriptures? Acts 17:11 - The Bereans eagerly received the message and studied the Scripture daily to see if what Paul and Silas said was true.

5. If we call Jesus our Lord, what should we do? Luke 6:46-49 - If we call Jesus our Lord, we should listen to His teachings and put them into practice so our lives are set on a solid foundation.

6. Describe what happens to the man who hears Jesus' words and puts them into practice. Luke 6:46-48 - The man who hears Jesus' words and puts them into practice is like a person building a house on a solid foundation. They can withstand life's storms without collapsing.

7. Describe what happens to the man who hears Jesus' words and does not put them into practice. Luke 6:49 - The man who hears Jesus' words but doesn't act on them is like a house built without a foundation—when storms come, it collapses and is destroyed.

8. If we hold to Jesus' teaching, what will happen? John 8:31-32 - If we hold to Jesus' teaching, we will know the truth, and the truth will set us free.

9. What is the proof of our love for Jesus? John 14:21, 23-24 - We show our love for Jesus by doing what He teaches. When we follow His instructions, Jesus will make Himself known to us.

APPLICATION & REFLECTION QUESTION

What did you learn from this lesson? How will you apply it to your life?

____

____

____

____

Chapter 6
Discipleship and Leadership

Lesson One:
The Call – Make Disciples

1. What did Jesus call his followers to do? Matthew 28:19 - Jesus called His followers to go everywhere, help others follow Him, and baptize them in the name of the Father, the Son, and the Holy Spirit.

2. What specifically did Jesus say we must do after baptizing a new believer? Matt 28:20 - Jesus said we must teach them to obey everything He commanded. As the word of God spread in Jerusalem during the first century, what was the result? Acts 6:7 - The result was that the number of disciples increased significantly, and many priests became obedient to the faith.

3. What did Paul command Timothy to do with the things he had been taught? 2 Timothy 2:2 - Paul commanded Timothy to pass on what he had learned to trustworthy people who would teach others.

4. What do each of these illustrations teach about discipleship? 2 Timothy 2:3-6

    * **Soldier**: Stay focused, disciplined, and loyal to your mission without getting distracted by worldly concerns.

    * **Athlete**: Follow the rules and stay committed to training to win the prize.

    * **Farmer**: Work hard and be patient, trusting that your efforts will produce a harvest in time.

5. What are the Scriptures helpful for? 2 Timothy 3:16 - The Scriptures are useful for teaching, correcting, rebuking, and training in righteousness.

6. How did Jesus say we can know we are truly a disciple? John 8:31 Jesus said we are truly His disciples if we remain faithful to His teachings.

7. How can disciples become like their teacher? Luke 6:40 - Disciples become like their teacher by fully training under them.

8. How does Jesus describe the person who hears his teaching and acts on it? Luke 6:48 - Jesus describes that person as a wise builder who built a house on a solid foundation, able to withstand storms.

9. How does he describe the person who hears and does not act on his teaching? Luke 6:49 - Jesus describes that person as a foolish builder who built a house without a foundation, which leads to its collapse when storms hit.

10. What has Christ called us to? Why? 2 Timothy 1:9 - Christ has called us to live a holy life because doing so will enable us to fulfill His purpose for our lives.

11. What does the Bible say about those who are "in Christ"? 2 Corinthians 5:17 - The Bible says those who are "in Christ" are a new creation. Their old life has been replaced with a new life.

APPLICATION & REFLECTION QUESTION

Describe in your own words what you think it means to be a disciple.

____

____

____

____

Lesson Two:
The Cost – Absolute Surrender

1. What three things did Jesus say all his disciples must do? Mark 8:34

    - Jesus said His followers must let go of their way, be willing to face challenges for Him, and follow His example.

2. How often should someone who wants to be a disciple take up their cross? Luke 9:23 They must take up their cross [be willing to face challenges for Him] daily.

3. How did Jesus compare discipleship to war? Luke 14:31-33 – Jesus compared discipleship to war, because just like a king must count the cost before going into battle, we must be ready to surrender everything associated with our carnal nature to follow Him.

4. What else did Jesus compare being a disciple to? Luke 14:28 - Jesus compared being a disciple to building a tower, you must count the cost before you enlist.

5. What should we do before we start "building"? Luke 14:28-33 - Before we decide to follow Jesus, we should think carefully about what it will take and be ready to put Jesus first, whatever the cost.

6. What does it mean to count the cost of being a disciple? - Counting the cost means evaluating and understanding the sacrifices, challenges, and commitment required to follow Jesus fully.

7. What has it cost you to follow Jesus? What are you willing to give up to follow him?

____

____

____

8. When it comes to discipleship, why is it so important to be able to finish what we start? Luke 14:29-30 - Finishing what we start is important because it demonstrates genuine commitment and faithfulness to Christ. Giving up can lead to personal regret and show others that our faith is not deeply rooted, potentially discouraging them from following Jesus.

9. Who cannot be a disciple? Luke 14:27,33 - Jesus said that you can't be His disciple, if you're not willing to face challenges for Him or put Him above everything else in your life.

APPLICATION & REFLECTION QUESTION

What did you learn from this lesson? How will you apply it to your life?

____

____

____

____

Lesson Three:
Discipleship and the Cross

1. What happened at the cross? Colossians 2:13-15 - At the cross, Jesus took on all our sins and paid the price for them so we could be forgiven and made right with God. He cancelled the "debt" we owed because of our mistakes and wiped our record clean. Jesus also defeated the power of sin, death, and evil, making sure that they no longer have control over those who trust in Him.

2. How did Paul describe his message to the Corinthians? 1 Corinthians 2:1-2 - Paul said he focused only on Jesus and His sacrifice, not on fancy words or human wisdom. What is the message of the cross to the perishing? What about those who are being saved? 1 Corinthians 1:18 - The cross seems pointless for those who don't believe. But for those who trust in Jesus, it reveals God's power to save.

3. What did Paul boast about? Galatians 6:14 - Paul boasted that Jesus' death on the cross saved us by defeating sin and freeing us from the world's control. What happened in Paul's life due to Jesus' death on the cross? Galatians 6:14 - Paul's life was changed because the world no longer controlled him; he now lived fully for Jesus.

4. What do you think Paul meant when he said, "I have been crucified with Christ"? Galatians 2:20 - Paul meant that his old self, ruled by sin, died with Jesus, and now he lives a new life through faith in Christ.

5. What did he mean by the phrase, "I no longer live, but Christ lives in me"? Galatians 2:20 - Paul meant that his life is no longer about his desires, but about fulfilling Jesus' purpose for his life.

APPLICATION & REFLECTION QUESTION

What do you think it means for you to be crucified with Christ?

____

____

____

____

Lesson Four:
Christian Character

1. What has God provided for us by his divine power? 2 Peter 1:3 - God has given us everything we need for a life of godliness, including the power to know Him and follow His ways.

2. How are we able to "participate in the divine nature"? 2 Peter 1:4 -We can participate in God's divine nature by trusting His promises. What can we escape as a result? 2 Peter 1:4 - We can escape the world's sin, corruption, and destructive desires.

3. What is the foundational "ingredient" to which everything else needed for a Godly life is added? 2 Peter 1:5 - The foundational ingredient is faith.

4. What are the necessary "additives" that Peter lists? 2 Peter 1:5-7 - The necessary additives are goodness, knowledge, self-control, perseverance, godliness, mutual affection and love.

5. What is the promised result of having these qualities in "increasing measure"? 2 Peter 1:8 - If we have these qualities in increasing measure, we will be productive and effective in knowing Jesus.

6. Describe the condition of those without these character qualities. 2 Peter 1:9 - Those who lack these qualities are spiritually blind and short-sighted, forgetting they have been forgiven of their sins.

7. What is the promise to those who develop this Christian character? 2 Peter 1:10-11 - Those who develop this Christian character will never fall away, and God will welcome them into His eternal kingdom.

8. Why should we rejoice in suffering? Romans 5:3-4 - We rejoice in suffering because it builds perseverance, which leads to character and, ultimately, to hope.

9. Why did James say we could consider trials "pure joy"? James 1:2-3 - James said we can consider trials "pure joy" because they test our faith, which builds perseverance and strengthens us.

10. What results in our lives when perseverance finishes its work? James 1:4 - When perseverance finishes its work, we become mature, complete, and lacking nothing.

APPLICATION & REFELECTION

What did you learn from this lesson? How will you apply it to your life?

____

____

____

____

Lesson Five:
Discipleship and Leadership

1. What did Jesus tell his first disciples to do? Matthew 4:19 - Jesus told His first disciples to follow Him, and He would teach them how to bring people to God.

2. What did Jesus promise he would do for his followers if they responded? Matthew 4:19 - Jesus promised to teach His followers how to reach and guide others to God.

3. How did the first disciples respond to Jesus' command and promise? Matthew 4:20 - The first disciples immediately left what they were doing and followed Jesus.

4. What did Jesus give his disciples the authority to do? Matthew 10:1

   - Jesus gave His disciples authority to drive out evil spirits, and heal every disease, and sickness. What did they do with that authority? Mark 6:7, 12-13 - The disciples went out in pairs, calling people to turn back to God and exercising authority by setting people free from evil spirits and healing the sick.

5. Did Jesus want his disciples just to follow him and watch him minister, or did he want them to watch, learn, and do all they saw him do? Jesus wanted His disciples to watch, learn, and do everything they saw Him do—continuing His work and helping others.

6. Are you in a discipleship group? Who is the leader? When and where does the group meet?

---

7. What did Jesus tell his disciples before he left Earth? Matthew 28:19 - Jesus told His disciples to go and make followers of all nations, baptize them, and teach them to follow His teachings.

8. What are we to teach the people we are discipling? Matthew 28:20

   - We are to teach them to obey everything Jesus commanded.

9. What is the difference between teaching facts and teaching someone to obey God's commands? Matthew 28:20 - The difference is that teaching facts focuses on sharing knowledge, while teaching obedience involves guiding someone to live out God's commands in their daily life through action and transformation.

10. What was Jesus' final promise to all who attempt to make disciples?

Matthew 28:20 - Jesus' final promise was, "I am with you always, even to the end of the age."

APPLICATION & REFLECTION QUESTION

What did you learn from this lesson? How will you apply it to your life?

____

____

____

____

Chapter 7
Spiritual Family and Church Life

Lesson One:
The Victorious Church

1. What did Jesus say about his victorious church? Matthew 16:18 - Jesus said His church will be strong and unstoppable, overcoming all evil.

2. Who is the "rock"? 1 Corinthians 10:4 - The "rock" is Christ Jesus.Who is the "chief cornerstone"? Ephesians 2:20 - The "chief cornerstone" isChrist Jesus.

3. What does Paul compare the love Christ has for the church to? Ephesians 5:25-28 - Paul compares Christ's love for the church to a husband's love for his wife.

4. How does Paul describe the ultimate destiny of the church? Ephesians 5:26-27 - Paul describes the church's destiny as holy, spotless, and radiant, presented to Christ without blemish.

5. What were the first church members devoted to? Acts 2:42 - The first church members were dedicated to teaching, fellowship, breaking of bread, and prayer.

6. Briefly describe early church life. Acts 2:42-47 -

7. vs. 43 - They experienced awe as miracles and signs were performed.

8. vs. 44 - Believers were united and shared everything in common.

9. vs. 45 - They sold their property and possessions to help those in need.

10. vs. 46 - They met daily in the temple and joyously shared meals.

11. vs. 47 - They praised God, gained favour with people, and God added new believers to the church daily.

12. Comment on the generosity of the early church. Acts 4:32-37 - The early church showed remarkable generosity by sharing everything they had. They sold property to ensure that no one among them lacked anything.

APPLICATION & REFLECTION

Are you part of a church community? If so, how is your church similar to the one described in Acts 2:43-47 and 4:32-37? How is it different? What can you learn from the early church?

____

____

____

____

Lesson Two:
The Body of Christ

1. What does Paul call the people of God in 1 Corinthians 12:27? - Paul calls the people of God "the body of Christ". This means believers are connected and work together like body parts, with Jesus as the head.

2. What does Paul say about the importance of each part of the body of Christ? 1 Corinthians 12:14-20 - Paul says that every part of the body of Christ is essential. No part can say it isn't needed. Just like a physical body needs all its parts to function, the church needs every believer to play their role. God has placed each person where they belong for a purpose.

3. Who decides how each part of the body should function? 1 Corinthians 12:21 - Paul teaches that God chooses how each part of the body should function.

4. What does Paul say to those who think they do not need the rest of the body? 1 Corinthians 12:21 - Paul says that no part of the body can say to another, "I don't need you." Every believer is essential, and we depend on each other in the body of Christ.

5. What does Paul say about the parts of the body "that seem to be weaker"? 1 Corinthians 12:22-24 - Paul says that the parts of the body that seem weaker are significant. God gives special honour to these parts, ensuring that every member of the body of Christ is valued and cared for.

6. How should the different parts of the body treat each other? 1 Corinthians 12:25-26 - Paul says the body of Christ should care for one another. If one part suffers, everyone suffers; if one part is honoured, everyone rejoices. We are called to support and love each other.

7. List the seven "ones" mentioned in Ephesians 4:4-6

   - One body

   - One Spirit

   - One hope

   - One Lord

   - One faith

   - One baptism

   - One God and Father of all

8. What should we do to maintain oneness or unity? Ephesians 4:3 - We should work hard to live in peace, be patient, and stay connected through the Holy Spirit.

9. What did Jesus pray for regarding the unity of his disciples? John 17:20-21 - He prayed for unity among all believers so that the world would believe God sent Him.

10. What does the Bible call someone who stirs up dissension- that is, who causes disunity? Proverbs 16:28 - Someone who stirs up dissension is a "perverse person" and a "gossip." Such a person spreads strife and separates close friends.

11. Proverbs lists seven things that are "detestable" to the Lord.

    What is the seventh? Proverbs 6:16-19 -The seventh

    thing detestable to the Lord is "a person who stirs up conflict in the community." God hates actions that cause division and harm relationships among His people.

APPLICATION & REFLECTION QUESTION

What role do you believe God is calling you to serve in His church? How has he gifted you? Try asking a Christian friend who knows you well what they think your gift might be.

____

____

____

____

Lesson Three:
Church Leadership

1. What five roles of authority and leadership did God place in the church? Ephesians 4:11 - Apostles, Prophets, Evangelists, Pastors, and Teachers.

2. What is the job of these leaders? Ephesians 4:12-13 -

- **Apostles – Sent by God to establish churches and spread the gospel in new areas.**

    - **Prophets – Speak God's message to encourage, correct, and guide the church.**

    - **Evangelists – Share the gospel and lead people to Jesus.**

    - **Pastors – Cares for the spiritual needs of believers.**

    - **Teachers – Instruct and help believers understand God's Word.**

3. How long will these gifts operate in the church? Ephesians 4:13 - These leadership gifts are meant to help the church grow until Jesus returns and we are fully transformed in Him.

4. What is the result of being in a church where these five ministries operate? Ephesians 4:14 - Believers stay grounded, grow deeper in faith, and avoid being misled.

5. How is the body of Christ "joined and held together"? Ephesians 4:16 - The body of Christ (the Church) is joined and held together through love, unity, and each believer doing their part.

6. Why was Titus left in Crete? Titus 1:5 - Titus was left in Crete to bring order to the church and appoint godly leaders.

7. Describe the qualifications for being an elder. Titus 1:6-9; 1 Timothy 3:2-7 - Character:

   - Blameless (above reproach) – A life of integrity, free from scandals.

   - Faithful to their spouse – A committed and honorable marriage.

   - Self-controlled – Not quick-tempered, reckless, or given to excess.

   - Sober-minded – Wise, sensible, and emotionally mature.

   - Not violent or quarrelsome – Peaceful, not abusive or argumentative.

   - Not greedy – Does not love money or seek dishonest gain. Family & Social Life

   - Manages their household well – Leads their family in a godly way.

   - Children are respectful and believe – Raises children in faith and discipline.

   - Hospitable – Welcomes and cares for others.

   - Respected by outsiders – Has a good reputation in the community. Spiritual Maturity & Teaching Ability

   - Loves what is good – Seeks righteousness and godly living.

   - Holds firm to sound doctrine – Faithfully teaches and defends the truth.

   - Able to teach – Explains Scripture clearly and applies it wisely.

   - Not a recent convert – Has spiritual maturity to avoid pride.

8. What do these passages teach about an elder's marriage, children, and home life? Titus 1:6-9; 1 Timothy 3:2-7 - An elder must be faithful to their spouse, lead their family well, and have children who respect them. If they can't manage their own home with love and discipline, they won't be able to lead the church effectively.

9. What was Peter's exhortation to the elders? 1 Peter 5:1-4 - Peter urged elders to care for God's people willingly and humbly, not for personal gain but as loving shepherds. He reminded them to lead by example, not by force and promised that when Jesus returns, they will receive a great reward.

APPLICATION & REFLECTION QUESTION

What did you learn from this lesson? How will you apply it to your life?

____

____

____

____

Lesson Four:
Church Discipline

1. What are some of the responsibilities of pastors, elders, and spiritual leaders?

   - John 21:15-17 – Feed and care for God's people with love.

   - Acts 20:28 – Watch over and protect the church as faithful shepherds.

   - Ezekiel 33:1-9 – Warn people of spiritual danger and guide them toward God.

   - Ezekiel 34:2-5 – Lead with love, not neglect or selfishness.

2. How should church members relate to their pastors, elders, and spiritual leaders?

   - 1 Thessalonians 5:12-13 – Respect and appreciate leaders for their hard work.

   - 1 Thessalonians 5:25 – Pray for spiritual leaders.

   - 1 Timothy 5:17-18 – Honour and support those who lead and teach well.

   - Hebrews 13:7 – Follow their example of faith.

   - Hebrews 13:17 – Obey and submit to their guidance, as they watch over our souls.

3. Who is the "head" of the church? Ephesians 4:15 - Jesus Christ is the Head of the Church.

4. What is the "foundation" of the church? 1 Corinthians 3:10-11 - The foundation of the church is Jesus Christ, and no other foundation can be laid apart from Him.

5. What should we do if we know a brother or sister has something against us? Matthew 5:23-24 - We should reconcile with them first, making peace before worshiping God.

6. What three steps should be taken to deal with sin in the church? Matthew 18:15-17

7. Matthew 18:15 – Speak to the person privately and try to resolve the issue.

8. Matthew 18:16 – If they don't listen, bring one or two others as witnesses.

9. Matthew 18:17 – If they still refuse to listen, bring it before the church, and if they reject correction, treat them as an outsider.

10. What should happen to the church member who is consistently wicked and immoral? 1 Corinthians 5:9-13 - The church should not associate with a member who is openly wicked and unrepentant. Remove them from fellowship if necessary, while leaving final judgment to God.

11. If we have no discipline, what are we? Hebrews 12:8 - If we have no discipline, it means we are not truly part of God's family.

12. What will we share in, as a result of this discipline? Hebrews 12:10 - Through God's discipline, we will share in His holiness and become more like Him.

13. What will this discipline ultimately produce? Hebrews 12:11 - God's discipline will eventually produce a harvest of righteousness and peace for those who accept it.

APPLICATION & REFLECTION QUESTION

What did you learn from this lesson? How will you apply it to your life?

____

____

____

____

Lesson Five:
Holy Communion

1. What were the early disciples devoted to? Acts 2:42 - The early disciples were devoted to the apostles' teaching, fellowship, and sharing meals. This included the Lord's Supper and prayer.

2. What is proclaimed when we have communion? 1 Corinthians 11:26 - When we take communion, we remember Jesus' death and declare our faith until He returns.

3. What are we guilty of if we receive communion in an "unworthy manner"? 1 Corinthians 11:27 - If we take communion without respect or a right heart, we disrespect Jesus' sacrifice.

4. What should we do before we receive communion? 1 Corinthians 11:28 - Before taking communion, we should think about our actions and attitude to ensure we are living in a manner that honours Jesus.

5. What happens to us if we continue to receive communion and do not turn from sin? 1 Corinthians 11:29 - If we take communion without turning from sin, we bring judgment on ourselves because we are not honoring Jesus' sacrifice.

6. What can happen as a result of this? 1 Corinthians 11:30 - As a result, some may become weak, sick, or even die because they do not respect the meaning of communion.

7. How can we avoid being judged? 1 Corinthians 11:31 - We can prevent judgment by honestly examining our actions and making things right with God.

8. When God judges or disciplines his children, what is his motive? 1 Corinthians 11:32 - When God disciplines us, His goal is to correct us and keep us from being condemned with the world.

APPLICATION & REFLECTION QUESTION

What did you learn from this lesson? How will you apply it to your life?

____

____

____

____

Chapter 8
Prayer & Worship

Lesson One:
Personal Prayer

1. When and where did Jesus pray? Mark 1:35 - Jesus prayed early in the morning, in a quiet place away from others.

2. Where do the hypocrites pray? Matthew 6:5 - The hypocrites pray in public places where others can see them because they want attention.

3. Where did Jesus teach his followers to pray? Matthew 6:6 - Jesus taught his followers to pray in a private place where they could be alone with God.

4. To whom did Jesus say we should pray? Matthew 6:6, 8-9 - Jesus said we should pray to God the Father because He knows our needs and listens to us.

5. What do the pagans think about prayer? Matthew 6:7 - The pagans believe repeating many words will make their prayers more effective.

6. What should we pray for? Matthew 6:9-13

    - vs. 9 - Pray to honour God's name.

    - vs. 10 - Pray for God's kingdom and His will to be done.

    - vs. 11 - Pray for daily needs.

    - vs. 12 - Pray for forgiveness and to forgive others.

    - vs. 13 - Pray for protection from temptation and evil.

APPLICATION & REFLECTION QUESTION

Think about the role prayer plays in your own life. Do you have a

specific time set aside for daily prayer? When? Do you have a private place for worship? Where?

____

____

____

____

Lesson Two:
The Power of Prayer

1. What does Jesus promise those who ask, seek, and knock? Matthew 7:7-11 - Jesus promises that if we pray and keep coming to God, He will answer us, and provide what we need. It's just like expecting someone to open a door when we knock.

2. What does Jesus say we must do for our prayers to be answered? Mark 11:24 - Jesus says we must believe that God will answer our prayers when we ask.

3. What can we receive if we pray and believe it? Matthew 21:22 - Jesus says that if we pray and believe, we will receive what we ask for.

4. What might be the reason we don't receive what we ask for? James 4:3 - We might not receive what we ask for if our motives are selfish or if we only want things for our pleasure.

5. What does Jesus teach us about prayer in the parable of the persistent widow? Luke 18:1-8 - Jesus teaches that we should always pray and not give up. The parable shows that if an unjust judge helped a persistent widow, how much more will God, who is loving and just, answer those who keep praying.

6. What can hinder our prayers?

    - Psalm 66:18-19 – God will not listen to our prayers if we hold on to sin in our hearts and refuse to turn from it.

    - James 1:6-8 – If we doubt God and lack faith, our prayers may not be answered.

    - 1 Peter 3:7 – If we treat others, especially our spouse, poorly, our prayers can be hindered.

7. In whose name should we pray? John 14:13-14 - We should pray in Jesus' name because He is the way to the Father, and He has the authority to answer prayers.

8. To whom should we present our requests? Philippians 4:6 - We should present our requests to God, with thanksgiving and trust.

9. How do we get to God? John 14:6 - We get to God through Jesus, because He is the way, the truth, and the life. No one comes to the Father except through Him.

10. How many mediators are there between God and us? Who is the mediator? 1 Timothy 2:5 - Jesus is the only mediator between God and us.

11. What is the confidence we have in prayer? 1 John 5:14-15 - Our confidence in prayer is that God hears us when we ask for anything according to His will.

12. What were the results of the disciple's prayers? Acts 4:31 - After the disciples prayed, the place where they were gathered shook. They were filled with the Holy Spirit, and they spoke God's word boldly.

13. What were Paul & Silas doing while in prison? Acts 16:25 - Paul and Silas were praying and singing hymns to God while in prison, and the other prisoners were listening.

14. What were the results of their prayers? Acts 16:26-34 - Due to their prayers, an earthquake shook the prison, opening all the doors and loosening the prisoners' chains. The jailer, fearing the prisoners had escaped, was about to take

15. his life, but Paul stopped him. The jailer and his family then came to believe in Jesus. They were baptized and filled with joy.

16. What was Elijah's prayer request and God's answer? James 5:17-18 - Elijah prayed that it would not rain, and God stopped the rain for three and a half years. Then he prayed again, and God sent rain to the land.

APPLICATION & REFLECTION QUESTIONS

What did you learn from this lesson about the power of prayer? How has God answered your prayers?

____

____

____

____

Lesson Three:
Corporate Prayer

1. What were the disciples doing as they waited for the day of Pentecost and the outpouring of the Holy Spirit? Acts 1:13-14 - The disciples were gathered together, praying constantly and united in faith as they waited for the Holy Spirit.

2. What did the believers do when they heard of Peter and John's arrest and persecution at the hands of the Sanhedrin? Acts 4:23-24

    - When the believers heard about Peter and John's arrest and persecution, they gathered together and prayed to God with one voice.

3. During the persecution, what were their prayer requests? Acts 4:29-30 - During the persecution, the believers prayed for boldness to preach God's Word and for God to perform healings, signs, and wonders through the name of Jesus.

4. What was the church doing while Peter was in prison? Acts 12:5,12

    - While Peter was in prison, and the church was earnestly praying for him.

5. How did God answer their prayers? Acts 12:7-12 - God sent an angel to Peter in prison. He woke Peter up, removed his chains, and led him past the guards and out of prison.

6. What were the Antioch church leaders doing when God called Saul and Barnabas to the mission field? Acts 13:2 - The Antioch church leaders were worshiping the Lord and fasting when God called Saul and Barnabas to the mission field.

7. What did they do before sending them off? Acts 13:3 - Before sending them off, the believers fasted, prayed, and laid their hands on Saul and Barnabas to commission them for their mission.

8. What is essential in corporate prayer? Matthew 18:19 - In corporate prayer, unity is vital. Jesus said that if two agree in prayer, God will answer.

9. What did Jesus promise? Matthew 18:20 - Jesus promised that when two or three gather in His name, He is there with them.

APPLICATION & REFLECTION QUESTION

What did you learn from this lesson? How will you apply it to your life? Do you have a community of believers with whom you can pray regularly?

____

____

____

____

Lesson Four:
A Biblical Prayer List

1. What was Paul's prayer for the disciples in Ephesus? Ephesians 1:17-

   - Ephesians 1:17 – Paul prayed that God would give them spiritual wisdom and revelation to know Him better.

   - Ephesians 1:18 – He prayed that their hearts would be enlightened to understand the hope and riches of their inheritance in Christ.

   - Ephesians 3:16 – He asked God to strengthen them with power through the Holy Spirit.

   - Ephesians 3:17-19 – He prayed that Christ would dwell in their hearts through faith, they would be rooted in love, and they would understand the depth of God's love.

2. What was Paul's prayer for the Philippian church? Philippians 1:9- 11 - Paul prayed that their love would grow in knowledge and wisdom, and they would be able to discern what is best and be pure and blameless, filled with the fruit of righteousness through Jesus Christ.

3. What was Paul's prayer for the Colossians? Colossians 1:9-12 - Paul prayed that the Colossians would be filled with the knowledge of God's will, have spiritual wisdom and understanding, live in a way that pleases the Lord, bear good fruit, grow in knowing God, be strengthened with His power, have endurance and patience, and give thanks for their inheritance in Christ.

4. What did Paul instruct the Colossians to pray for? Colossians 4:2-4 - Paul instructed the Colossians to be devoted to prayer, to stay watchful and thankful, and to pray that God would open doors for the gospel so he could share the message of Christ.

5. What was Epaphras always doing for the Colossians? Colossians 4:12 - Epaphras was always praying for the Colossians, asking God to help them stand firm and follow His will.

6. What was Paul's prayer request to the Thessalonian believers? 2 Thessalonians 3:1-2 - Paul asked the Thessalonian believers to pray that the Lord's message would spread quickly and that he and his team would be rescued from evil people.

7. What was Paul's prayer for Philemon? Philemon 4-6 - Paul prayed with gratitude for Philemon, asking that his faith would deepen his understanding of every good thing he had in Christ.

APPLICATION & REFLECTION QUESTION

What did you learn from this lesson? How will you apply it to your life? What does your prayer list look like compared to the lists of Paul and the early believers?

____

____

____

____

Lesson Five:
Worship

1. What kind of people is God seeking? John 4:23 - God is seeking people who worship Him in spirit and truth.

2. How should we worship God? John 4:24 - We should worship God in spirit and in truth.

3. What does God say about using physical idols, statues, and images in worship? Deuteronomy 5:8-10 - God commands us not to make or worship idols, statues, or images, because He is a jealous God who desires our complete devotion.

4. What are we discouraged from doing? Hebrews 10:24-25 - We are encouraged not to stop meeting together with other believers, but to encourage one another and motivate each other toward love and good deeds.

5. What internal attitudes make our worship acceptable to God? Hebrews 12:28-29 - Our worship is acceptable to God when we approach Him with gratitude, reverence, and awe, recognizing His holiness and power.

6. What are some external expressions of worship encouraged in Scripture?

    - Psalm 47:1, 5-6 – Clapping hands, shouting joyfully, and praising God.

    - Psalm 96:8-9 – Bringing offerings, worshiping with reverence, and bowing before the Lord.

    - Psalm 98:1, 4-6 – Singing a new song, shouting for joy, and using instruments like harps and trumpets in praise.

    - Psalm 149:3 – Praising God with dancing and making music with instruments.

    - Psalm 150:3-6 – Worshiping with various instruments, loud praise, and everything that has breath giving praise to God.

7. In what two places did the early churchmen gather for worship and prayer? Acts 2:46; Acts 20:20 – They gathered in the temple courts and their homes for prayer and fellowship.

APPLICATION & REFLECTION QUESTION

What did you learn from this lesson? How will you apply it to your life? In what ways do you express your love for God?

____

____

____

Chapter 9
Faith & Hope

Lesson One:
What is Faith?

1. Faith is one of the few words that the Bible defines for us. What is faith? Hebrews 11:1 - Faith is confidence in what we hope for and assurance about what we do not see.

2. How does faith come to us? Romans 10:17 - Faith comes from listening to God's message as it is conveyed to us through the words of Christ.

3. How does faith express itself? Galatians 5:6 - Faith expresses itself through love.

4. What do the following verses teach about faith?

    *   Galatians 2:16 – We are made right with God through faith in Jesus Christ, not by following the law.

    *   Galatians 3:11 – No one is made right with God by the law. The righteous live by faith.

    *   Galatians 3:26 – Through faith in Christ Jesus, we become children of God.

    *   What is the foundation that must be laid in the life of every believer who

    *   wants to go on to maturity? Hebrews 6:1-2 - The foundation includes:

- Repentance from sin, faith in God, teachings about baptisms, laying on of

- hands, resurrection of the dead, and eternal judgment.

5. Who are we to put our faith in? Galatians 2:16 - We are to put our faith in Jesus Christ because we are made right with God through faith in Him, not by following the law.

6. After Thomas finally believed, who did Jesus say would be blessed? John 20:29 - Jesus said that those who believe without seeing will be blessed.

7. What should we do when our senses contradict our faith? 2 Corinthians 5:17 - We should live by faith, not by what we see or feel.

APPLICATION & REFLECTION QUESTION

What are some things you are sure of but do not see (e.g. air, North Pole, God, etc.)?

____

____

____

____

Lesson Two:
Saving Faith

1. What did Paul and Silas tell the jailer he had to do to be saved? Acts 16:30-31 - Paul and Silas told the jailer to place his trust in Jesus, and He would save him.

2. What did Paul tell the Romans they needed to do to be saved? Romans10:9-10 - Paul told the Romans they needed to believe in their heart that God raised Jesus from the dead and confess with their mouth that Jesus is Lord.

3. How are we justified? Romans 5:1 - We are justified by faith, which means God accepts us because we trust Jesus. The simple answer: We are made right with God by trusting in Jesus.

4. What is the result of our justification? Romans 5:1 - Because of faith, we are made right with God. Now we have peace with Him through Jesus.

5. How can we have access to God's grace? Romans 5:1-2 - We receive God's grace by putting our faith in Jesus.

6. Are people justified before God by obeying the law or putting their faith in

7. God? Romans 3:28 - People are made right with God through faith, not by obeying the law

8. Who does God justify? Romans 3:26 - God makes right anyone who trusts in Jesus.

9. How does righteousness come? Romans 3:22 - Righteousness comes by believing in Jesus.

10. How do the righteous live? Romans 1:17 - Those made right with God live by trusting Him.

11. Paul spoke of a righteousness that did not come from the law. Where did it come from? Philippians 3:8-9 - It comes from God when we put our faith in Jesus, not by keeping the law.

12. How are we saved? Ephesians 2:8 - We are saved by God's grace when we put our faith in Him. It's a gift from God, not something we earn.Who has the right to become "children of God"? John 1:12 - Those who receive Jesus and believe in Him can become children of God.

13. Who will not perish but have eternal life? John 3:16 - Anyone who believes in Jesus will have eternal life.

APPLICATION & REFLECTION QUESTION

What did you learn from this lesson? How will you apply it to your life?

____

____

____

____

Lesson Three:
Faith and Obedience

1. What does James say about faith that is not accompanied by action? James 2:17 - Faith without action isn't genuine—it's lifeless.

2. Is just saying that we believe in God enough? James 2:19 - Just saying you believe in God isn't enough—even demons believe He exists. Genuine faith is proven by how you live.

3. What are all people called to do? Romans 1:5 - We are all called to trust God and obey Him.

4. What did Abel do "by faith"? Hebrews 11:4 - Abel showed his faith by presenting to God a sincere sacrifice.

5. God called Abraham to a place he had never seen. What did Abraham do "by faith"? Hebrews 11:8 - Abraham trusted God and followed Him, even though he did not know the destination.

6. When God tested Abraham, what did he do "by faith"? Hebrews 11:17 - Abraham trusted God so profoundly that he was willing to give up his son.

7. After growing in the lap of luxury as the son of Pharaoh's daughter, what did Moses do "by faith"? Hebrews 11:24-25 - Moses refused to be known as the son of Pharaoh's daughter. He chose to be mistreated along with the people of God rather than to enjoy the fleeting pleasures of sin.

8. What else did Moses do "by faith"? Hebrews 11:27-28 - Moses trusted God by leaving Egypt and obeying God's instructions to protect His people.

9. What did all the Israelites do "by faith"? Hebrews 11:29 - The Israelites trusted God by walking through the Red Sea, believing He would make a way.

10. What happened in Jericho because of the Israelites' obedient faith? Hebrews 11:30 - By faith, the walls of Jericho fell after the army had marched around them for seven days.

11. Is it possible to be a man or woman of great faith and die without receiving what has been promised? Hebrews 11:37-39 - Yes, it is possible to be a man or woman of great faith and die without receiving what was promised.

12. What does it mean to love God? 1 John 5:3 - To love God means obeying what He says—not out of duty, but out of relationship and trust.

13. Are God's commands a burden? Why or why not? 1 John 5:3 - God's commands are not a burden. Because when we love God, obeying Him feels natural and joyful.

14. How does John describe faith? 1 John 5:4 - Faith provides us strength to win life's battles.

15. Who overcomes the world? 1 John 5:5 - All who believe that Jesus is the Son of God.

APPLICATION & REFLECTION QUESTION

How has your faith in God led to faithfulness? What did you learn from this lesson? How will you apply it to your life?

____

____

____

____

Lesson Four:
Mountain-Moving Faith

1. The disciples once failed to cast out a demon and asked Jesus, What was the reason they couldn't drive it out? Matthew 17:20 - Jesus said they couldn't cast out the demon because of their lack of faith.

2. Even if we have small faith in a big God, what can we do? Matthew 17:20 -Even if you have a little faith in a big God, nothing is impossible!

3. What was Abraham fully persuaded of? Romans 4:21 - He trusted that God is able to keep His word.

4. Some people ignore or deny the facts in a vain attempt to move in faith. What did Abraham do regarding the physical facts? Romans 4:19 - He didn't let the facts weaken his faith. He trusted God despite the physical facts.

5. What were the facts in Abraham's case? Romans 4:19 – Abraham was about One hundred years old, and Sarah's womb was dead.

6. What did Abraham not do when he faced the facts? Romans 4:20

7. - He never stopped believing. He grew stronger in his faith and worshipped God.

8. Why were Abraham and Sarah able to become parents? Hebrews 11:11 - They placed their faith in God.

9. What promise had God made to Abraham? Genesis 15:4-6 - God promised Abraham that he would have a son of his own, and his descendants would be as numerous as the stars.

10. In Ephesians, 6:10-17 Paul calls for believers to put on the "full armour of God." What can the shield of faith do? Ephesians 6:16 - Faith protects us from fiery darts [lies, fear, and attacks] from the enemy.

11. Who should we have faith in? Mark 11:22 - We should have faith in God.What must we do if we want our "mountain" to be thrown "into the sea"? Mark 11:23 - This is metaphorical language - we must speak to the mountain,

12. believe without doubting, and trust that it will happen.

APPLICATION & REFLECTION QUESTION

How have you seen the power of faith demonstrated in your own life? In the lives of others?

____

____

____

____

Lesson Five:
- Faith and Hope

1. What must we believe about God in order to come to him? Hebrews 11:6 - We must believe God exists, and He rewards those who sincerely seek Him.

2. What is impossible without faith? Hebrews 11:6 - Without faith, it is impossible to please God.

3. What is the connection between faith and hope? Hebrews 11:1 - Faith is being confident that what we hope for will happen, even if we can't see it yet.

4. What did the writer of Hebrews call hope? Hebrews 6:19 – The writer of Hebrews called hope an anchor for the soul, strong and secure.

5. What is the purpose of an anchor in a boat? - It keeps the boat secure.

6. How does hope anchor our soul? What happens to a person who has no hope? - Hope anchors our soul by keeping us steady and secure during hard times. It reminds us that God's promises are true. A person with no hope can feel lost, discouraged, and unsure about the future.

7. Faith deals with today, hope with tomorrow. What are we now by faith? 1 John 3:2 - By faith, we consider ourselves God's children, even if we don't fully understand what we will become.

8. What will happen to us when Jesus appears - that is, what is our hope? 1 John 3:2 - When Jesus appears, we will become like Him.

9. How should this hope of seeing Jesus affect our lives? 1 John 3:3 - This hope should encourage us to live pure lives.

APPLICATION & REFLECTION QUESTION

What did you learn from this lesson? How will you apply it to your life?

____

____

____

____

Chapter 10
Biblical Prosperity and Generosity

Lesson One:
The Dangers of Wealth

1. According to Jesus' parable of the sower, what can choke out God's word and cause it to be unfruitful? Mark 4:18-19 - In the parable of the sower, Jesus said that the worries of life, the desire for wealth, and the pursuit of other things can choke out God's word, making it unfruitful. These distractions can take our focus away from God and prevent us from growing spiritually.

2. What are some ways people are deceived by wealth?

    * False Security: Wealth can create a false sense of security, leading us to trust

    * in our resources rather than in God.

    * Divided Loyalties: It can tempt us to prioritize possessions over relationships and purpose.

    * Misplaced Identity: Wealth can subtly convince us that our value is tied to what we own, rather than who we are in Christ.

    * Spiritual Blindness: It can blind us to the needs of others and the call to generosity.

3. What are some worries of life that choke out God's word? Matthew 6:25, 28, 31,34 -

    * Worry About Daily Needs (v. 25) – Concerns about food, drink, and clothing can distract us from trusting God's provision.

- Worry About Physical Appearance (v. 28): Anxiety over outward appearance can distract us from inner spiritual growth.

- Worry About the Future (v. 31, 34): Fear of the unknown and the pressures of tomorrow can overwhelm our present well-being.

4. Is it impossible to serve both God and wealth? Luke 16:13. Yes.

5. What can happen to those eager for money and who want to get rich? 1 Timothy 6:9-10 - People who want to get rich can fall into temptation and traps that lead to pain and regret. Loving money can cause people to turn away from their faith and experience great sorrow.

6. Do you want to get rich? What are some of the potential dangers of this desire?

   Personal answer ____

7. What is the root of all kinds of evil? 1 Timothy 6:10 - A love for Money.

8. What can deliver us from death, righteousness or money? Proverbs 11:4 Trusting in money leads to failure, but living a righteous life leads to safety and life.

9. What happens to those who trust in money? Proverbs 11:28 - People who trust in money will end up in trouble, but those who do what is right will have a good and healthy life.

10. Do riches last? Proverbs 23:4-5 - Riches can disappear quickly, like an eagle flying away, so don't wear yourself out trying to get them.

11. What should we guard ourselves against? Luke 12:15 - We should guard against greed, because life isn't measured by how much we own.

12. Read Luke 12:16-21. What is the point of the parable of the rich fool? - Jesus warns that focusing on wealth without thinking about God is foolish. The rich man stored up wealth for himself but ignored his spiritual life, and lost everything when he died. The lesson is that true life is about being rich toward God, not just gathering possessions.

APPLICATION & REFLECTION QUESTION

What did you learn about the dangers of money?

Lesson Two:
Biblical Principles of Prosperity

1. Who gives us the ability to produce wealth? Deuteronomy 8:18 - God is the one who provides us with the ability to produce wealth.

2. Read Deuteronomy 30:8-10. What did Moses tell the Israelites God would do for them if they obeyed his commands? - He would bless their work, make them prosperous, and give them success in everything they did.

3. What do the following verses from Proverbs have to say about prosperity or God's provision?

   • Proverbs 10:3 – God provides for the needs of the righteous but lets the wicked go hungry.

- Proverbs 10:4 – Hard work leads to wealth, while laziness brings poverty.

- Proverbs 10:22 – The blessing of the Lord makes a person rich, and it comes without sorrow.

- Proverbs 13:21 – Trouble chases sinners, but good things happen to the righteous.

- Proverbs 13:22 – A good person leaves an inheritance for their children, but sinners' wealth is stored up for the righteous.

- Proverbs 21:21 – Pursuing righteousness and love leads to life, prosperity, and honour.

- Proverbs 22:4 – Humility and the fear of the Lord bring wealth, honour, and life.

- Proverbs 22:9 – Generous people will be blessed because they share their food with the poor.

4. What happens when we give? What if we give a small measure? What if we give with a large measure? Luke 6:38 - When we give, we receive in return. If we give a little, we receive a little, but if we give generously, we receive generously.

5. How does the "law of sowing and reaping" apply to money? 2 Corinthians 9:6 - Just like a farmer who plants more seeds obtains a bigger harvest, being generous leads to more incredible blessings.

6. What kind of giver does the Lord love? 2 Corinthians 9:7 - God loves people who give cheerfully, not because they have to, but because they want to.

7. What can God do for the cheerful giver? 2 Corinthians 9:8 - God can give them everything they need and more than enough so they can keep doing good for others.

8. Why does God make people rich? 2 Corinthians 9:11 - God makes people rich so they can be generous, which, in turn, brings thanksgiving and praise to God.

APPLICATION & REFLECTION QUESTION

How has God blessed you with abundance? How can you use that abundance to bless others?

____

____

____

____

Lesson Three:
Putting God First

1. What did the Israelites do with the first portion of all God provided for them? 2 Chronicles 31:5-6 - The Israelites brought the first part of their crops, herds, and flocks as an offering to God. They gave generously and faithfully to support God's work.

2. What part should we give to God? Proverbs 3:9 - We should honour God by giving Him the first and the best part of everything we have.

3. What happens as a result of giving the first part to God? Proverbs 3:10 - God will bless us with more than enough to meet our needs.

4. Leviticus 27:30-32. Should we give a tithe of everything or only our net pay? On the first part or the leftover part? Before or after taxes and other expenses? - The Bible teaches that we should give a tithe (10%) of everything God gives us, and it should be the first part, not the leftovers. This means giving before spending on other things, as a way to put God first and trust Him to provide.

5. Why did Malachi tell God's people they were under a curse? Malachi 3:9 - Because they were not giving their tithes and offerings. They were robbing God by keeping what belonged to Him.

6. How do people rob God? Malachi 3:8 - By not giving their tithes and offerings —the portion that belongs to Him.

7. How did God tell them to test Him? Malachi 3:10 - God told them to bring the full tithe into the storehouse and test Him to see if He would open the windows of heaven and pour out more blessings than they could hold.

8. What did God promise to do if his people would give him the whole tithe? Malachi 3:10-12 -

- Give them more blessings than they could hold.

- Protect what they worked for, like their jobs or income.

- And make others see how blessed they are and want what they have.

APPLICATION & REFLECTION QUESTION

What did you learn from this lesson? How will you apply it to your life?

____

____

____

____

Lesson Four:
Extreme Generosity

1. According to Jesus, who gave the most? Luke 21:1-4 - Jesus said the poor widow gave the most because she gave all she had, while others gave only a tiny part of their wealth.

2. Paul bragged about the generosity of the Macedonian believers. Describe their situation. 2 Corinthians 8:2 - The Macedonian believers were impoverished and going through hard times, yet they were joyful and gave generously, even beyond what they could afford.

3. How much did the Macedonians give? 2 Corinthians 8:3 - They gave as much as they could—And even more than that, giving freely and willingly.

4. Did Paul have to pressure the Macedonian believers to give? What was their attitude toward giving? 2 Corinthians 8:4 - Paul didn't have to pressure them—instead, they begged for the chance to give. They saw it as a privilege to help others.

APPLICATION & REFLECTION QUESTION

What did you learn from this lesson? How will you apply it to your life? What kind of giver are you?

_______________________________Less than you can afford.

_______________________________As much as you can afford.

_______________________________More than you can afford.

Chapter 11
Evangelism and World Missions

Lesson One:
Everyone Is a Minister

1. What "ministry" has God given to each believer? 2 Corinthians 5:18

   - God has given each believer the ministry of helping people be made right with God through Jesus Christ.

2. What "message" has God committed to us? 2 Corinthians 5:19 - God has committed to us the good news that He wants to restore our relationship with Him through Christ.

3. What does reconciliation mean, and why do people need to be reconciled to God? - Reconciliation means restoring a broken relationship. People need to be reconciled to God because our sin has placed a barrier between us and a Holy God.

4. What is an ambassador? An ambassador is a person who represents another country or organization in a foreign place. In the Bible, it means we represent Christ's message of reconciliation to those who are broken by sin.

5. What does it mean for us to be Christ's ambassadors? 2 Corinthians 5:20 - Being Christ's ambassadors means we speak on His behalf, urging others to be reconciled to God, just like He would if He were here in person.

6. How will other people know that we are followers of Jesus? John 13:35 - People will know we are followers of Jesus by the love we show to one another.

7. What was Paul's attitude toward sharing the gospel with non-Christians? Romans 1:14-16.

    - vs. 14 – Paul felt obligated to share the gospel with everyone, no matter who they were.

    - vs. 15 – He was eager to preach the gospel to people in Rome.

    - vs. 16 – He was not ashamed of the gospel because it is God's power to save everyone who believes.

8. What must happen for people to "call on the name of the Lord"? Romans 10:14-15 - People can only call on the name of the Lord if they believe in Him. They can't believe unless they hear about Him, and they can't hear unless someone tells them.

9. God sent Peter to preach the gospel to a Roman centurion named Cornelius. Who did Cornelius gather to hear Peter preach? Acts 10:24 - Cornelius gathered his relatives, his servants and close friends to hear Peter preach the gospel.

10. What happened to those who heard Peter preach in Cornelius's house? Acts 10:44-48 - The Holy Spirit came upon all who listened to the message. They began to speak in tongues and praise God, and then they were baptized in the name of Jesus Christ.

11. Where did Paul preach? Acts 20:20 - Paul preached publicly and from house to house.

12. To whom did Paul preach? Acts 20:21 - Paul preached to both Jews and Greeks.

13. What did Paul preach? Acts 20:21 - Paul preached that people must repent (turn) to God and have faith in the Lord Jesus Christ.

APPLICATION & REFLECTION QUESTION

What did you learn from this lesson? How will you apply it to your life? With whom - friends, loved ones, or even enemies - is God calling you to share the gospel?

____

____

____

____

Lesson Two:
Boldness

1. Under the threat of persecution, what did the disciples pray for? Acts 4:29 - Under the threat of persecution, the disciples prayed for boldness to speak God's word.

2. What were the results of their prayer? Acts 4:31 - After they prayed, the place where they were meeting shook, they were all filled with the Holy Spirit, and they spoke God's word boldly.

3. According to Barnabas, how did Saul (Paul) preach - even in the face of a plot to kill him? Acts 9:22-28 - According to Barnabas, Saul (Paul) preached boldly in the name of Jesus, even though people were planning to kill him.

4. After Saul's conversion, how long did he wait until he preached the gospel? Acts 9:19-20 - Saul began preaching about Jesus just a few days after his conversion.

5. Describe the difference between a righteous man and a wicked man. Proverbs 28:1 - A good person stands firm and confident, but someone doing wrong lives in fear even when there's no reason to.

6. What does Proverbs say about those who fear other people? Proverbs 29:25 - Proverbs says that being afraid of people can trap you, but trusting God keeps you safe.

7. Paul requested prayers that he might preach the gospel in what manner? Ephesians 6:19-20 - Paul asked for prayers so he could preach the gospel boldly and clearly, without fear.

APPLICATION & REFLECTION QUESTION

What did you learn from this lesson? How will you apply it to your life? Take a moment to ask God to give you boldness to share the message of salvation with others.

____

____

____

____

Lesson Three:
Spiritual Conflict and Evangelism

1. What has happened to unbelievers? 2 Corinthians 4:4 - Unbelievers have been blinded by the god of this world (Satan) so they can't see the truth about Jesus and His message.

2. How are people taken captive? Colossians 2:8 - People are taken captive by false ideas and human traditions that are not based on Christ.

3. What did Jesus come to do? Luke 4:18-21 - Jesus came to bring good news to the poor, heal the brokenhearted, free the captives, give sight to the blind, and set the oppressed free.

4. Why did the Son of God appear? 1 John 3:8 - To destroy the works of the devil.

5. Who are we struggling against? Ephesians 6:12 - We are struggling against the spiritual forces of evil, not people, but the devil's forces.

6. What happened when Paul preached? Acts 16:14 - When Paul preached, Lydia's heart was opened to receive Christ.

7. What must happen if people are to come to Christ? John 6:44 - People can only come to Christ if God the Father draws them to Him.

APPLICATION & REFLECTION QUESTION

What did you learn from this lesson? How will you apply it to your life?

____

____

____

____

Lesson Four:
Miracles, Signs, and Wonders

1. When the disciples stepped out in faith and boldly preached the gospel, what happened? Acts 2:43; 3:16 - When the disciples boldly preached the gospel, miracles happened, people were filled with awe, and a man was healed through faith in Jesus' name.

2. Why did the people in Samaria pay close attention to Philip? Acts 8:6-8 - The people in Samaria paid close attention to Philip because they saw miracles, heard him speak about Jesus, and many were healed and set free joy filled the city.

3. What were Paul & Barnabas doing when the lame man from Lystra was healed? Acts 14:5-10 - They were sharing the gospel with a group of people.

4. What did James instruct the church to do for those who were sick? James 5:14-15 - James instructed the church to call the elders to pray over the sick person and anoint them with oil in the name of the Lord.

5. What did Jesus promise to those with faith? John 14:12 - Jesus promised that those who believe in Him will do the same works He did—and even greater ones.

6. How can we see "even greater things"? John 14:12-14 - We can see even greater things by believing in Jesus and praying in His name.

7. How was the crippled man at the Beautiful Gate healed? Acts 3:6-7, 16 - The crippled man was healed through faith in the name of Jesus.

8. How much authority is in the name of Jesus? Matthew 28:18 - All authority in heaven and on earth has been given to Jesus.

9. What happens at the mention of Jesus' name? Philippians 2:10-11 - At the name of Jesus, every knee will bow in heaven, on earth, and under the earth, and every tongue will confess He is Lord.

10. What did Jesus say would happen if we have faith in Him? Mark 11:23-24 - Jesus said that if we really believe and don't doubt, amazing things can happen—even things that seem impossible.

11. What did Jesus say about the power of faith? Mark 9:23 - Jesus said that anything is possible if you believe.

12. What pleases God? Hebrews 11:6 - Our faith in his word.

APPLICATION & REFLECTION QUESTION

How have you seen the power of God at work in your life? Think of a time when you boldly proclaimed the gospel. How did God act?

____

____

____

____

Lesson Five:
To the Ends of the Earth

1. What did Jesus promise would happen when the Holy Spirit came on his followers? Acts 1:8 - Jesus promised that when the Holy Spirit came on His followers, they would receive power and be His witnesses everywhere.

2. What is a witness? - A witness is someone who tells others what they have seen, heard, or experienced.

3. What does it mean to be Christ's witness? - To be Christ's witness means to share with others what Jesus has done in your life and to help them know who He is.

4. Where were Jesus' followers to be witnesses? Acts 1:8 - Jesus' followers were to tell people about Him in their city, in the nearby regions, and all over the world.

5. What was the first promise Jesus gave to his followers? Matthew 4:19 - Jesus promised that if they followed Him, He would teach them how to bring others to God.

6. What was the last command Jesus gave to his disciples? Matthew 28:19 - Jesus' last command was to go and make disciples of all nations.

7. What are we to do with the disciples we make? Matthew 28:19-20 - We are to baptize them and teach them to obey everything Jesus taught.

8. What did Jesus promise to everyone who would go and make disciples of all nations? Matthew 28:20 - Jesus promised that He would be with us always, even to the end of time.

9. What is the condition of the world in relation to the gospel? Matthew 9:35-37; John 4:35-36 - The world is full of people ready to hear the gospel, like a field ready for harvest, but there aren't enough workers to share the message.

10. What did Jesus say we should pray for? Matthew 9:38 - Jesus said we should pray for more workers to go out and share the good news with others.

11. Jesus died on the cross to purchase people from where? Revelation 5:9 - Jesus died to purchase people for God from every tribe, language, people, and nation on the earth.

APPLICATION & REFLECTION QUESTION

What did you learn from this lesson? How will you apply it to your life? What part is God calling you to play in fulfilling his command to reach every nation with the gospel?

____

____

____

____

Chapter 12
Resurrection and Judgment

Lesson One:
Death and Resurrection

1. What is everyone appointed to do once? Hebrews 9:27 - Everyone is appointed to die once.

2. Where will we all stand one day? Romans 14:10 - Before Christ to be judged for how we lived our lives.

3. Did Paul fear death? Why not? Philippians 1:21 - Paul wasn't afraid of dying because he believed living meant serving Jesus, and dying would be even better since he'd be with Jesus.

4. What did Paul say to those who said there is no resurrection? 1 Corinthians 15:13 - Paul said that if there is no resurrection, then not even Christ has been raised.

5. What if Christ was not resurrected? 1 Corinthians 15:14-19

    - vs. 14 – Our preaching and faith would be useless.

    - vs. 15 – We would be lying about God, saying He raised Christ when He didn't.

    - vs. 16 – If the dead aren't raised, then Christ hasn't been raised either.

    - vs. 17 – If Christ wasn't raised, our faith is worthless, and we're still in our sins.

- vs. 18 – Those who have died believing in Christ will be lost forever.

- vs. 19 – If our hope in Christ is only for this life, we are to be pitied more than anyone.

6. What is the last enemy Christ will destroy? 1 Corinthians 15:26 - Death.

7. How did Paul describe the resurrection body? 1 Corinthians 15:42- 44

- vs. 42 – It is raised to last forever, not to die again.

- vs. 43 – It is raised in glory and power, not weakness or dishonour.

- vs. 44 – It is a spiritual body, not just a natural one.

8. Paul did not relate to Jesus as if he were still on the cross. How did Paul want to know Christ? Philippians 3:10 - He desired to know Him in the power of His resurrection.

9. What did Paul hope to attain? Philippians 3:11 - Paul hoped to attain the resurrection from the dead, so he could live forever with Christ.

10. What was Paul's hope? Acts 24:15 - Paul was confident that both the righteous and the unrighteous would be raised from the dead.

11. How did Paul's belief in the resurrection affect the way he lived? Acts 24:16 - Paul worked hard to keep his conscience clear before God and people.

12. Where is our citizenship? Philippians 3:20 - Our citizenship is in Heaven.

13. What will our Saviour do to our bodies? Philippians 3:21 - Jesus will transform our weak, earthly bodies to be like His glorious body.

14. To be alive in the body is to be away from the Lord - 2 Corinthians 5:6.

15. To be away from the body is to be at home with the Lord - 2 Corinthians 5:8.

16. Where must we all appear one day? 2 Corinthians 5:10 - We must all appear before the judgment seat of Christ.

17. Why did Jesus share in our humanity? Hebrews 2:14 - Jesus shared in our humanity so that by dying, He could destroy the devil, who holds the power of death.

18. Who holds the power of death? Hebrews 2:14 - Satan held the power of death before Christ's resurrection.

19. Who broke his power? How? Hebrews 2:14 - Christ broke his power through his death and resurrection.

20. Is it possible to be set free from the fear of death? How? Hebrews 2:15 - Yes, we can be free from the fear of death as we place our faith in Jesus. He destroyed its power.

APPLICATION & REFLECTION QUESTION

What did you learn from this lesson? How will you apply it to your life?

____

____

____

____

Lesson Two:
The Justice of God and the Sinfulness of Humanity

1. What is the foundation of God's throne? Psalm 89:14 – The foundation of God's throne is righteousness and justice.

2. What if we claim to be a Christian yet walk in darkness? 1 John 1:6 - If we claim to be Christians but live in darkness, we are lying and not living by the truth.

3. What if we claim to be without sin? 1 John 1:8 - If we claim to be without sin, we are deceiving ourselves and the truth is not in us.

4. What if we deliberately continue to sin? Hebrews 10:26-27 - If someone knowingly and stubbornly keeps choosing sin after understanding the truth about Jesus, they are rejecting the only way to be forgiven. This isn't about someone who struggles or makes mistakes—it's about someone who turns their back on Jesus and refuses to repent. The warning is meant to wake us up, not push us away. If we turn to God with a sincere heart, He will always forgive us. (1 John 1:9).

5. What do you think it means to trample on the Son of God and insult the Spirit of grace? Hebrews 10:28-29 - It means treating Jesus' sacrifice as worthless and ignoring or rejecting the Holy Spirit's offer of forgiveness. It's like turning your back on God's love after fully knowing what Jesus did for you. It's a severe warning not to take His grace lightly.

6. Why is it a dreadful thing to fall into the hands of the living God? Hebrews 10:30-31 - God is holy and just. He sees everything, and He will judge those who reject Him and His grace.

7. What are those with stubborn, unrepentant hearts doing? Romans 2:5 - They are storing up God's anger. He will judge them severely on the day of judgment.

8. What can those who reject God's truth expect from Him? Romans 2:8 - Those who reject God's truth can expect anger and punishment because they choose to do evil instead of obeying Him.

9. What do those who believe in Jesus have? What about those who reject Jesus? John 3:36 - Those who believe in Jesus will have eternal life. But those who reject Him won't have life, and God's judgment stays on them.

10. How are those who believe in Jesus to speak and act? James 2:12 - Those who believe in Jesus should speak and act like people who know they'll be judged by God's law of love and freedom.

11. What if we live a pretty good life and do our best to follow God, but disobey just once? James 2:10 - If we disobey just once, it's as if we've broken the whole law.

12. What is the moral condition of every human? Romans 3:23 - Every human has sinned and falls short of God's perfect standard.

13. How can we be justified before God? Romans 3:24 - We can only be justified before God by His grace, through the gift of salvation that comes by Jesus Christ.

14. What did the sacrificial death of Christ demonstrate? Romans 3:25-26 - The sacrificial death of Christ showed that God is fair and just. It proved He punishes sin but also forgives those who trust in Jesus.

15. God is not only just, but He is also the one who makes right everyone who puts their trust in Jesus. Romans 3:26.

APPLICATION & REFLECTION QUESTION

What did you learn from this lesson? How will you apply it to your life?

____

____

____

____

Lesson Three:
The Judgment of Sinners

1. What comes after death? Hebrews 9:27 - We will face judgment.

2. Who will enter the kingdom of heaven? Matthew 7:21 - Only those who do what God wants, and those who obey His will shall enter the kingdom of heaven.

3. What will Jesus say to those who called him Lord but did not live under his Lordship? Matthew 7:22-23 - Jesus will say He never knew them. He will tell them to go away because they practiced evil instead of obeying Him.

4. On judgment day, Jesus will separate the "sheep from the goats" - that is, the righteous from the wicked. What are the only two eternal destinations after judgment? Matthew 25:46 - Heaven, which is eternity in God's Kingdom, and Hell, which is eternal separation from God.

5. How is hell described in the following passages?

- Matthew 13:41-42 – A fiery furnace with weeping and grinding of teeth.

- Matthew 25:41 – Eternal fire prepared for the devil and his angels.

- Mark 9:43 – Unending fire that never goes out.

- Luke 16:23-24 – A place of torment, burning, and great suffering.

- 2 Thessalonians 1:9 – Eternal separation from God's presence and His power.

6. Who will be judged in hell?

- Matthew 23:29-33 – Hypocrites and those guilty of rejecting God's messengers.

- Matthew 24:48-51 – Wicked, unfaithful servants who live selfishly and harm others.

- John 3:36 – Those who reject Jesus and do not believe in Him.

- Romans 2:8 – Those who are selfish, reject the truth, and do evil.

- Revelation 20:15 – Anyone whose name is not written in the Book of Life.

- Revelation 21:8 – The cowardly, unbelieving, vile, murderers, sexually immoral, those who practice witchcraft, idolaters, and liars.

7. What do the following Scripture passages teach about the "fear of God"?

- Deuteronomy 10:12 – Fear God by loving Him, serving Him, and obeying His commands.

- Ecclesiastes 12:13 – Fearing God and keeping His commands is the whole purpose of life.

- Isaiah 8:13 – Fear God as the holy one we should honour and respect.

- Matthew 10:28 – Fear God, who has power over both body and soul after death.

- Luke 1:50 – God shows mercy to those who fear Him.

- Acts 10:35 – God accepts people from every nation who fear Him and do what is right.

APPLICATION & REFLECTION QUESTION

What did you learn from this lesson? How will you apply it to your life? How do you "fear God" in your everyday life?

____

____

____

____

Lesson Four:
The Judgment of Saints

1. What does Jesus do for us? 1 Thessalonians 1:10 - Jesus rescues us from the coming judgment and punishment.

2. What did Paul tell the believers in Rome? Romans 14:10-12 - Paul told the believers that everyone will stand before God and give an account of their own life.

3. What did Paul tell the believers in Corinth? 2 Corinthians 5:10 - Paul said we will all appear before Christ to be judged for what we've done, good or bad.

4. What will the fire test on judgment day? 1 Corinthians 3:13 - God will test what each person has done to see if it was excellent and lasting — works motivated by love for God and others.

5. What will we receive if our work survives God's judgment? 1 Corinthians 3:14 - If our work survives, we will receive a reward from God.

6. What if our life's work is burned up in judgment? 1 Corinthians 3:15

   - If our work is burned up, we will lose the reward, but we will still be saved — like someone barely escaping a fire.

7. What did James say about the judgment of spiritual leaders? James 3:1 - James said spiritual leaders will be judged more strictly.

8. What did David say about the death of those who are faithful to the Lord? Psalm 116:15 - David said the death of those faithful to the Lord is precious in God's sight.

9. What did John say about the death of a believer? Revelation 14:13- John said believers who die are blessed and will rest from their work, and their good deeds will follow them.

10. What must we believe about God? Hebrews 11:6 - We must believe that God exists and that He rewards those who sincerely seek Him.

11. Athletes in ancient Rome competed for crowns made of perishable materials, such as leaves and vines. What kind of crown does the Christian train for? 1 Corinthians 9:25 - Christians train for a crown that will last forever.

12. What were Paul's thoughts about the possibility of making it to heaven (by the grace of God) only to be disqualified from

13. receiving "the prize"? 1 Corinthians 9:26-27 - Paul disciplined himself and stayed focused, so he wouldn't be disqualified and lose his reward.

14. What was Paul's "crown"? Philippians 4:1 - Paul's crown was the people he led to Christ, the believers who stood firm in their faith.

15. What was Paul's "hope," his "joy," his "crown"? 1 Thessalonians 2:19 - Paul's hope, joy, and crown were the people who would stand before Jesus at His coming because of his ministry.

16. Who will be rewarded with the "crown of righteousness"? 2 Timothy 4:7-8 - The crown of righteousness will be given to all who have stayed faithful and who look forward to Jesus' return.

17. Paul says the Crown of Righteousness is for those who long for Jesus' return. According to Peter, what should those who "look forward to the day of God do"? 2 Peter 3:11-12 - Peter said that those who look forward to the day of God should live holy and godly lives.

18. What reward does God give those who persevere under severe trials? James 1:12 - God gives the crown of life to those who stay strong under trials and love Him.

19. What must we be to receive the "victor's crown"? Revelation 2:10 - We must remain faithful, even if it means facing death.

20. What activities does God promise to reward?

- Matthew 6:3-4 – God will reward giving to others in secret.

- Matthew 6:6 – God will reward those who pray in private.

- Matthew 6:16-18 – God will reward fasting done quietly and sincerely.

21. Revelation 4 describes four living creatures who circle the throne of God, worshipping day and night. What do these heavenly beings do with their crowns? Revelation 4:9-10 - The heavenly beings lay their crowns before God's throne to honour and worship Him.

22. Why is God worthy of our crowns? Revelation 4:11 - Because He created everything, and everything exists by His will.

APPLICATION & REFLECTION QUESTION

What did you learn from this lesson? How will you apply it to your life?

____

____

____

____